WEST OF IRELAND SUMMERS

A Cookbook

WEST OF IRELAND SUMMERS

A Cookbook

TAMASIN DAY-LEWIS

PHOTOGRAPHY BY SIMON WHEELER

PHOENIX ILLUSTRATED

This book is for the friends and family I have cooked for over the years, and will continue to do so with as undimmed a passion in the future. Cooking for them is one of the great pleasures in life, and should never be underrated. I hope this book will reflect some of that pleasure to them and everyone who reads it.

First published in 1997 by
George Weidenfeld & Nicolson

This paperback edition first published in 1999 by
Phoenix Illustrated
Orion Publishing Group
Orion House
5, Upper St. Martin's Lane
London WC2H 9EA

ISBN: 0753806959

Designed by Nigel Soper
Edited by Maggie Ramsay
Photographs by Simon Wheeler

Contents

CHAPTER 1
Childhood Summers 7

CHAPTER 2
Return to the West 43

CHAPTER 3
My House in Mayo 59

CHAPTER 4
Local Food 79

CHAPTER 5
Entertaining 99

CHAPTER 6
Christmas in the West 115

CHAPTER 7
Chocolate and Mad March Hares 127

CHAPTER 8
Inish Turk and Favourite Food 141

Recipe Index 160

CHAPTER 1

Childhood Summers

I cannot imagine my earliest childhood memories revolving around anything other than food, cooking and kitchens. I remember the intense hunger of childhood, the excitement of smelling and tasting things for the first time. The extraordinary pleasure of being allowed to pick my grandfather's grouse bones, of tomatoes from the greenhouse in my grandparents' kitchen garden, which provided one delight after another: baby carrots freshly dug; the first asparagus; squeaky peas laced with butter, cream, sugar and mint; tiny pebbles of new potatoes; warm raspberries.

It is easy to feel nostalgia for the food of one's childhood: the comfort, anticipation, newness, and sometimes forbiddenness of late-night raids on the fridge, midnight feasts, and things bought secretly because they weren't allowed. There was the fascination with other people's food (the things one never got at home), and the fact that other people's picnics were always more delicious

My daughter Charissa on the beach.

Childhood summers. Dan and I with our parents.

than one's own. Curiosity about the actual cooking came later. Apart from the usual childhood attempts at biscuits, cakes and gruesomely grey and leaden pastry, I was content to think, dream and eat food rather than help make it. A decade of west of Ireland summers changed all that.

The first year our parents took us, I was nine years old. The tub that bucketed across the Irish Sea overnight from Liverpool had us rolling around below sea level in a tiny cabin, with me begging to be allowed up on deck to smell the salt, freeze in the wind and tramp about whey-faced to allay the nausea. The treat at the end of the journey was a night at The Russell Hotel in Dublin, where Seamus the barman made my father the best whiskey sours in Ireland.

We began our holiday at Ballyconneely in Connemara, and then drove round Killary Bay to Mayo, to Old Head Hotel in Clew Bay. Old Head was a sprawly, shambolic family hotel, approached by a long track flanked by dense hedges laden with rosehips, buzzing with wasps and bees. The hallway was all threadbare carpets, scratching dogs, fishing rods and gumboots.

It was presided over by one of the most unlikely figures ever to become a hotelier. Alec Wallace had read, among other things, Latin, Greek, Philosophy and Mathematics at Trinity College, Dublin, and had come back to the west to run the hotel after his father died. In the early days of us holidaying there, Alec's awesome mother, Mrs Wallace, terrorized kitchen staff, maids and guests alike. Her recipes were handed down first to Margaret the cook, and then, I imagine, from Margaret to Dympna, who ruled the kitchen after Margaret left. Excitable, loud and prone to fits of hysterical laughter, Dympna managed to keep sane and unfazed whatever the heat in the kitchen.

The food at Old Head was about as reliable as the Irish weather. It could be sublime or abysmal or both together. Much depended on the catch. Very often Dympna did not know what she'd be cooking for dinner until Alec came in with it. He kept his lobster pots in Clew Bay, and we'd go out in his little boat and haul them up, often finding vicious catfish rather than crabs and lobsters. In August the mackerel would follow the dolphins into the bay, and you'd only have to hang a line of hooks near the boat to have half a dozen of the petrolly-glazed fish thrashing on the line. Dan and I used to sell them at Old Head quay for a penny each. Sea trout were plentiful then, as were bottom fish such as turbot and skate, but, more than anything, I remember the freshly caught wild salmon, shimmering silver in their gluey skins, strong-bodied, lean-tailed, with their signature smell, unlike any other, when they'd been hauled out of the water after their final fight. That and the local lamb are the smells I associate with the Old Head kitchen.

Thirty years ago exotic fruit and vegetables had been neither seen nor heard of in the west of Ireland. Turnip, carrot, cabbage and potatoes were the staples, along with pallid oranges, apples, pears and bananas. So we ate stews and roasts and damply delicious cakes of soda bread, followed by old-fashioned nursery puddings. After a day braced against the Atlantic winds and waves, such was the craving for carbohydrates that guests were expected – indeed encouraged – to ask for second helpings. If the weather was too abysmal to picnic, we'd brave the dining room for a disguised rerun of the night before. Huge tureens of last night's lamb cooked with macaroni and tomato sauce, or floury-potatoed Irish stews, were consumed in epic quantities.

Looking back on a decade of childhood summers, I am struck most by how they elide into one collective memory. If Alec asked Dan out fishing on one of the loughs, I would ride the beaches on whatever animal I could borrow. There was one year that stands out from the rest. I had been riding a beautiful horse that belonged to the local butcher. I was asked if I would like to ride her in the local races down at Carrownisky Strand. Fear didn't enter into it. I was 13, too young to think of caution or consequences. I was introduced to my trainer Louis Heneghan who knew a lot about horses. There was a huge double field surrounded by banks where Louis schooled me. Mainly I remember him lying on one of the banks reading huge tomes for his law degree. On the day of the races the whole of Carrownisky Strand was covered in tinkers' stalls, bookmakers and a huge crowd of drinking men and large families. The opposition were all male, all tough local farmers.

My mother, clearly agitated, was begging my father not to let me ride – or so I presume. I would certainly have the same fear for my three children. I knew by the look my father shot me that we had a tacit understanding, he could see the horse and I were safe, sharing the same purpose, and that he wouldn't stop me.

One horse leapt ahead of the starting gun, we all followed; clearly there was no turning back as we thrashed it out across the sand. Another horse ran out and headed straight for the sea, the rest of us hugged together into a

Me on Lonisburgh Lass, Carrowniskky Strand.

tight knot until the end when one horse made a spurt for the finish. I came second. Honour was satisfied. Louis and I now remain friends, as do our families. His youngest son is pictured on his new horse at Old Head (see page 126). My father's poem preserves the moment:

Remembering Carrownisky

THE TRAIN window trapped fugitive impressions
As we passed, grasped for a moment then sucked away
Woods, hills, white farms changing shape and position,
A river which wandered, as if not sure of the way,

Into and off the pane. A landscape less
Well-groomed than, say, a Florentine painter's one,
But its cross-rhythmed shagginess soothed me through the glass
As it ambled past out there in the setting sun.

Then, one Welsh mead turned up with a girl rider
Light hair, red jersey – cantering her horse
Momently creatures out of some mythical order
Of being they seemed, to justify and endorse

A distrait mood… I recalled you at thirteen
Matched against Irish farmers in a race
On Carrownisky – under the cap your dark mane
Streaming, the red windcheater a far-off blaze;

But most how, before the race began, you rode
Slowly round the circuit of sand to calm
The mare and accustom her to a lawless crowd.
Seeing that, I knew you should come to no harm.

Our nerves too can taste of our children's pure
Confidence and grow calm. My daughter rides back
To me down the railside field – elemental, secure
As an image that time may bury but not unmake.

Charissa in one of the ruins at the deserted Derry village.

It was about that time that Alec took on several local girls to work at Old Head who have remained friends ever since. Merci O'Malley arrived with her brother Richard and cousin Evelyn. Evelyn was a bit older than us, and better versed in what dance happened in what dance hall on what night of the week. Dan and I met their brothers, sisters, cousins, friends – who were also usually related as is the way in such a community. Most nights we'd meet up in town and every so often the word would get out – barbecue on the beach tonight. They seemed to have a curious life of their own, people would emerge from the shadows with food, drink, turf for the fire, guitars for music, and we'd all sit out until the small hours in a curious glow of excitement, dreaminess – not wanting the magic to end.

It was as much of an annual ritual every Christmas when Papa would turn to Dan and me and ask us where we wanted to spend the next summer. I'm sure it was a secret pleasure of his to know the answer would always be Mayo. Coxes, Keanes, Sammins, O'Malleys, we look back with them now at a row of perfect summers, and wonder as does every generation whether our children could ever have such fun.

Whether it is something in the climate of the west or a factor that defies analysis I do not know, but it is a place that induces a semi-permanent carbohydrate-crazed appetite in our family, the same now as it was in our childhood. I suspect it is the combination of ocean, wind-battered beaches, granite mountains and extreme exercise, which all conspire with the damp, salty air to make one long for hearty soups and stews, slabs of bread and dense, filling cakes. Mediterranean cuisine has a place, a very small place, on the sudden glorious days in July or August, those damp, warm-sun days when you can picnic until the early evening chill descends, always well before supper time.

So the natural food to start with has to be some of the warming dishes that would be more likely to be served in winter anywhere else, but in Ireland one eats all year round.

FROM LEFT TO RIGHT: *Harry, Charissa, John Kilcoyne, me, Miranda and Merci Kilcoyne.*

Beef Braised with Guinness

Serves 6–8

2 tbsp olive oil
1.5 kg/3 lb chuck steak, cut into large cubes and trimmed
1 large onion, chopped
450 g/1 lb carrots, cut into fingers
6 cloves garlic, peeled but left whole
2 tbsp plain flour
1 tbsp tomato purée
750 ml/1¼ pints Guinness
1 bouquet garni with 3 bay leaves, 2 sprigs of rosemary, thyme and parsley and 3 strips of orange peel, tied together with string
salt and pepper

Optional:
200 g/7 oz prunes, soaked overnight and drained (preferably left whole)

Everyone has their own version of carbonade of beef. This is mine, one I have been making since I first left home and learned to cook. It is a richly dark stew, with the slight bitterness of the Guinness sweetened and scented by the orange peel and rosemary. The prunes are optional, but they will flavour and enrich the dish. I like to serve this with two traditional Irish accompaniments, Baked Onions and Colcannon (see overleaf).

Preheat the oven to 150°C/300°F/Gas Mark 2. Heat the oil in a heavy-bottomed casserole and seal the meat briefly on all sides. Remove with a slotted spoon and put to one side. Add the onion, carrots and garlic and let them begin to colour before sprinkling them with the flour. Add the tomato purée, stir and then return the meat to the casserole. Pour in the Guinness slowly, stirring and allowing the liquid to thicken. Bury the bouquet garni in the liquid and bring to boiling point. Season and put into the oven for 1½ hours.

Add the soaked prunes if you are using them, and cook for a further 30 minutes. When the meat is tender, remove and discard the bouquet garni and serve hot, with Baked Onions and Colcannon.

Ingredients for beef braised with Guinness.

Baked Onions

Allow 1 large onion per person. Trim the bases if necessary so that they will stand upright, but do not peel. Stand the onions in a roasting tin and pour in about 2.5 cm/1 inch of hot water. Bake at the same time as the beef (see page 12). Serve the onions in their skins, with butter and salt.

Colcannon

SERVES 6–8

1 kg/2½ lb green cabbage, finely chopped
2 small leeks, finely chopped
150–300 ml/^{1}5–10 fl oz milk
1 kg/2½ lb potatoes, roughly chopped
salt and pepper
pinch of grated nutmeg
125 g/4 oz butter, melted

The Irish make this with kale, but it's just as good with cabbage.

Simmer the cabbage and leeks in just enough milk to cover, until soft. Boil the potatoes until tender, drain and mash them, then season to taste with salt, pepper and nutmeg. Add the cabbage, leek and milk mixture. Place in a deep, warmed serving dish, make a well in the centre and pour in the melted butter. Serve the vegetables with spoonfuls of the butter.

Irish Stew

SERVES 4–6

2 tbsp olive oil
4 onions, sliced
2 cloves garlic, crushed
1 kg/2½ lb small potatoes, or chopped larger ones
1 kg/2½ lb middle neck of lamb, in cutlets
1 bouquet garni with 2 bay leaves, 2 sprigs of rosemary, thyme and parsley, tied together with string
1.5–1.7 litres/2½–3 pints chicken stock
200 g/7 oz barley
450 g/1 lb carrots, thinly sliced
3 sticks of celery, sliced
a handful of fresh parsley, chopped
salt and pepper

There are surely as many recipes for this stew as there are people to eat it, and purists would frown at mine, but the Irish stew of my childhood always had barley in it and that's how I like it. A wonderful one-pot meal.

Heat the oil in a large, heavy-bottomed casserole and add the onions, garlic and half the potatoes. Cook over a low heat until the onions are slightly softened. Add the lamb, bouquet garni and the stock and bring to boiling point, then simmer for 20 minutes.

Add the barley and continue simmering for 10 minutes, then add the carrots, celery, half the chopped parsley and the remaining potatoes. Simmer for a further 30 minutes, by which time the lamb should be tender and the first lot of potatoes and the barley will have thickened the stew. Season to taste, add the remaining parsley and serve in bowls.

Baked onions.

Alec also ran Delphi Lodge at Lough Doo, a 20-minute bone-shaker of a ride through the mountains from Old Head, where the serious fishing fraternity stayed. In those days it was frequented by English and Irish grandees and Nobel prizewinners. Both would ask Alec to dine with them, and he would be infinitely courteous on both occasions, but it was the Nobel bunch with whom he felt most comfortable. He would have sped the shellfish – normally scuttling across the back seat of his Mini – to Delphi, where the cook would set to work with an even tighter deadline than Old Head's. What you caught, you gave to the cook, who happily prepared it for you – from lough to table in a matter of hours. Guests poured drinks for themselves and signed for them, turf fires smouldered darkly, the lights flickered more than the fires, and Alec had to wait up for the last guest to go to bed before he turned off the generator and the whole place was plunged into darkness.

The first chance I had to see the real miracle of hotel catering was the year I went to Old Head to barmaid for Alec. I was 15, and happy to work 16 or more hours a day, six days a week, for £5 plus tips. After bottling up and making the guests' lunches, my real education got under way in the bar. Alec would talk about Shakespeare, Marlowe (whom he really believed *was* Shakespeare), Sir Walter Raleigh and the School of Night; about writers as yet unknown to me such as T. F. Powys and Thomas Lovell Beddoes; about the history of mathematical notation; about whatever he was reading in Marsh's Library – all in Greek and Latin – in Dublin where he wintered out.

At midnight, local culture resumed. A group of friends, all working at Old Head, would hitch in to the dances at the parochial hall, or the Starlight ballroom in Westport; William Trevor's *Ballroom of Romance* said it all. The girls jived together until the sober-suited men crossed the floor to the girls' side for a dance. Basil and the Beat Minstrels filled the air. We'd fall into bed in the early hours, to be revived at dawn by Dympna's breakfast: fresh eggs from the hens, strong salty rashers, Castlebar sausages, black pudding and tomatoes. We sat in the kitchen while Dympna made batches of biscuits and cakes for the teas, the rest of us wilting at her frenetic cutting, shaping and kneading. The kitchen window was held open against the heat by an industrial jam tin, in which the wasps would drown in a sea of sweetness. Under the sink were the slop buckets for the pigs – nothing was wasted; today's hygiene inspectors would be pole-axed with horror and close the place down immediately. We all helped do everything and the kitchen taught me organization, speed, and how all food has two lives: what you intended it for in the first place and its second incarnation as a 'leftover' – in a sense the most creative form of cooking.

I have always loved puddings, and old Mrs Wallace had three outstanding recipes which we prayed would come round again every week. I finally got the recipe for two of them, but the deliciously honeyed, spiced, curranted Canadian Pie is still only a distant memory. I adapted the following two from the originals and cook them regularly. They are much loved by every child I have ever fed them to!

OVERLEAF: *The view across Lough Doo which means, literally, 'the dark lake'.*

Butterscotch Tart

SERVES 6

Shortcrust Pastry (see page 158), made with wholemeal flour
200 g/7 oz muscovado sugar
250 ml/8 fl oz single cream
85 g/3 oz butter
50 g/2 oz cornflour, sifted
3 egg yolks

MERINGUE TOPPING:
3 egg whites
50 g/2 oz caster sugar

A meltingly gooey tart; you can add chopped pecan nuts to the filling if you wish, and serve it with or without its meringue topping. Either way it is best served warm with single cream.

Preheat the oven to 200°C/400°F/Gas Mark 6. Roll out the pastry and use to line a 22 cm/9 inch tart tin with a removable base; chill for at least 20 minutes. Meanwhile, put the muscovado sugar, cream, butter, cornflour and egg yolks in a double boiler and whisk over a low heat until thick, creamy and lump free.

Bake the pastry blind for 10 minutes. Turn the oven down to 180°C/350°F/Gas Mark 4. Remove the greaseproof paper and beans and return the pastry to the oven for 5 minutes.

To make the meringue, whisk the egg whites until stiff, add one-third of the caster sugar and whisk again until stiff. Fold in another one-third of the sugar with a metal spoon. Pour the filling into the pastry case and spread the meringue mixture on the top. Scatter the remaining sugar over the meringue and return the tart to the oven for at least 20 minutes, until pale brown and crisp on the top.

Tasmanian Lemon Pie

SERVES 4–6

125 g/4 oz butter, softened
275 g/10 oz vanilla caster sugar (sugar that has been stored with a vanilla pod)
4 eggs, separated
4 tbsp plain flour, sifted
400 ml/14 fl oz milk
grated rind and juice of 2 lemons

This is one of those marvellously tangy puddings whose light sponge top conceals a lemon-curd-like, barely set bottom.

Preheat the oven to 180°C/350°F/Gas Mark 4. Cream the butter with the sugar until light and fluffy. Beat in the egg yolks, then the flour and milk, a little at a time. Add the grated rind and juice of the lemons. Whisk the egg whites until stiff and add to the mixture, folding lightly to incorporate air into the mixture. Pour into a greased baking dish, so the mixture comes about 5 cm/2 inches up the side of the dish. Cook in the oven for about 25–30 minutes, until slightly brown on top and obviously set but faintly shuddery. Serve warm with clotted cream.

The house at Tully.

The best teas I have eaten anywhere took place at Tully, a little over a mile away from Old Head. The Harmans were old friends of my parents, their gracefully shabby white house approached by the most beautiful avenue of palely pink, gaunt sycamore trees I have ever seen. The Bunowen river rushes past the house, so close to the drawing room that when it floods it has been known to alter its course, sending a tributary through the house.

Sally Harman was always good with children and animals. Dan and I would fish or swim in the bog-black Bunowen from the steps by the house, then emerge soaking into the fishing room, where guests' salmon and tackle, gaffs and gumboots, huge nets and scales to weigh the catch with kept everything chaotic, cluttered and fishy smelling. After eyeing the catch, we'd tiptoe into the kitchen, where Mary the cook guarded the range.

I have never seen such cakes as Mary's: high-rise cherry, the fruit firmly sunk to the bottom, Madeira with a hint of lemon rind, heavy fruit cakes, cakes of soda bread, cold curls of salted butter, and whitecurrant or blackcurrant jelly, loganberry and damson jams. The table would be ceremoniously laid, here and there silver jam spoons and teapots and knives, and Sally and her dogs would preside over a feast which still fills me with nostalgia and desire. We would sit and eat piece after piece of bread, butter and jam, one of the greatest combinations of all time if each one is of the highest quality, and then move on to the cakes, crisp and crumbly without, moist and fruity within.

I originally found Sally's husband forbidding. Sir Charles was an English High Court judge, toweringly huge, bespectacled, and always in the long tweed shorts that he fished in, but in fact he was funny and gentle and extremely kind to me and my brother.

Nearly 30 years later I took my children to tea with Sally – my son called her his oldest friend immediately, and she called him her youngest – she was 90 at the time.

When Sally died, it was the end of an era. We'd all told her how we expected to be having tea with her when she was 100. The whitecurrant bushes, the raspberry canes and the Irish Peach trees – my favourite variety of apple, little known, intensely flavoured – were places we wandered to on our way upstream to the turnpike, in anticipation of their transformation into Tully tea.

OVERLEAF: *The drive at Tully with its 150-year-old avenue of sycamores.*

Blackcurrant or Whitecurrant Jelly

Use 325 g/12 oz granulated sugar to each 450 g/1 lb of fruit. Put the currants, along with their stalks and leaves, into a large pan. Add the sugar. Bring to the boil, skimming off the scum as it comes to the surface, then boil fast for 10 minutes. Pour into a bowl through a hair or nylon sieve. Press the fruit down lightly – not firmly, or the jelly will cloud. Pour it warm into sterilized jam jars and seal. The blackcurrant jelly is wonderful in puddings, particularly queen of puddings.

Loganberry Jam

Whenever possible I prefer not to boil berries for fools, ice creams and, in this case, jam. The minimal cooking naturally results in a wonderfully intense flavour. It works just as well for raspberries.

Preheat the oven to 180°C/350°F/Gas Mark 4. Put equal weights of loganberries and granulated sugar in a large dish in the oven. Let them get very hot, but do not allow to boil. Check after 20 minutes, although it could take 30 minutes.

Turn the fruit and sugar into a bowl and mix together thoroughly with a wooden spoon. Pour warm into sterilized jam jars and cover with discs of paper that you have first dipped in brandy, then seal. If mould forms on top of the jam, don't worry; the jam underneath will be fine, and it keeps extremely well.

The soda breads overleaf are the best I know. Both recipes were given to me by one of my friends from Old Head days – she was working there the same summer I was – Merci Kilcoyne. Her husband John runs a large mussel-fishing business and co-operative in Killary Bay, working in unimaginably difficult weather on his mussel rafts. He takes a loaf with him every day!

Merci's soda bread.

Brown Soda Bread

MAKES A 450 G/1 LB LOAF

175 g/6 oz coarse (stoneground) wholewheat flour
275 g/10 oz wholewheat flour (organic if possible)
1 heaped tsp bicarbonate of soda
1 tsp salt
1 tsp molasses sugar
25 g/1 oz butter
500–600 ml/16–20 fl oz buttermilk

Preheat the oven to 230°C/450°F/Gas Mark 8. Mix all the dry ingredients together with your hands, lightly rubbing in the butter. Make a well in the centre and add about 500 ml/16 fl oz of the buttermilk. Working with a knife, from the centre, gather the mixture to make a soft, wet dough. You may have to add more buttermilk to make the mixture 'sticky wet'.

Grease a 450 g/1 lb round or oblong loaf tin, spoon in the dough and bake for 30 minutes. Cover the top with greaseproof paper and bake for a further 10–15 minutes. Turn out on to a wire rack and cover with a tea towel. Leave to cool slightly before attempting to slice the bread.

Anne Bourke's soda bread, Bourke's delicatessen, Bridge Street, Westport.

John's Bread

MAKES A 450 G/1 LB LOAF

325 g/12 oz strong unbleached white flour (organic if possible)
50 g/2 oz wholewheat flour
50 g/2 oz bran
25 g/1 oz butter
1 heaped tsp bicarbonate of soda
1 tsp sea salt
1 tsp molasses sugar
500–600 ml/16–20 fl oz buttermilk

The method and baking time are exactly as for the Brown Soda Bread (see opposite).

Madeira Cake

MAKES AN 18 CM/7 INCH ROUND CAKE

175 g/6 oz butter, softened
175–200 g/6–7 oz caster sugar
3 large eggs, beaten
225 g/8 oz plain flour, sifted
1 tsp baking powder
2 tbsp milk
grated rind of 1 lemon
caster or icing sugar
strips of lemon rind

This is the classic recipe. For cherry or fruit cakes, add 225 g/8 oz glacé cherries or mixed dried fruit.

Preheat the oven to 160–180°C/325–350°F/Gas Mark 3–4. Grease and flour an 18 cm/7 inch round cake tin. Cream the butter with the sugar until soft and light – the larger amount of sugar gives the cake a very fine texture. Gradually beat in the eggs. Fold in the flour and baking powder, then the milk and the lemon rind.

Spoon the mixture into the cake tin and bake for 35–40 minutes, then, if the cake is getting too brown, cover the top with greaseproof paper. If you like a moist cake, test (by inserting a skewer into the centre) after a further 40 minutes; if you prefer a slightly drier cake, give it 50–55 minutes. Leave to cool in the tin for a couple of minutes, then turn out on to a wire rack and leave to cool completely.

Decorate with caster or icing sugar and a couple of strips of lemon rind.

When Alec sold Old Head Hotel, a decade of wonderful summers was over. He began rebuilding an old ruin of a house further down the hill on the shoreline. It looked straight across Clew Bay to the holy mountain, Croagh Patrick, known locally as The Reek and made sacred by Saint Patrick. There is an annual pilgrimage up it every summer, the most stalwart scaling it barefoot to the chapel at the top.

Alec planted a kitchen garden that defied belief. Potatoes, carrots and cabbages vied for space with the exotic: Florentine fennel, aubergines, herbs, garlic, sorrel, artichokes, and a wonderful crop of oyster mushrooms from the dead oak tree he left lying horizontal by the drive.

In the evenings we recreated some of the dishes Alec had eaten on his travels through Turkey, Iran and Afghanistan: bulgar wheat salad with finely minced onion, tomatoes, cucumber and mint stirred in with lemon juice and olive oil; *ful medames*, the Egyptian brown beans with cumin and fresh coriander; cabbage leaves wrapped dolmades-style around spiced minced lamb with raisins and pine nuts.

In the mornings we'd experiment with the soda bread, baking spinach or carageen seaweed into it. But the real experimenting was with fish.

At night we'd go down to the beach with torches and watch for the little bubbling airholes in the sand that mean razor-fish. Plunging our arms into the wet sand as high to the elbow as we could, we'd grab the shells and wriggle them slowly and gently to the surface – one sharp move and the suckers and shells would separate and all would be lost. Arms scarred by the gritty sand, we'd take our spoil back to Boathaven to turn into razor-fish stew the following day.

In another experiment, Alec had punctured holes in a large metal biscuit tin, and I found him laying oak chips on the base of it and trying to get them to light. You could barely see across the kitchen for smoke. We decided on a brilliant combination: we'd smoke mussels with wild rice. I cooked the wild rice, and took the top shell off scores of barely cooked mussels. The mussels were extracted, the rice bed laid, the mussels put back with their juice, and laid on a rack in the tin. The lid was closed. We lit the touch paper and retired . . . The result was extraordinarily delicious, the oak-scented mussels and nutty rice a brilliant hors d'oeuvre

At the foot of Croagh Patrick.

with a glass of cold white wine.

We were forever catching unwanted fish when we went out on Alec's boat – by unwanted, I mean the sort we weren't looking for at the time. Pollack was one of them. Pollack, once you've extracted oceans of bones, is perfectly edible, but it is better married with a couple of other fish. I devised a fish pie which is, to my mind, the absolute best of its kind.

Scallop, Pollack and Squid Pie

SERVES 6

This combines the best qualities of nursery food with the sophistication and subtlety of a dish that can be served at a dinner party.

1 kg/2½ lb pollack, skinned and filleted
300–450 ml/10–15 fl oz milk
1 kg/2½ lb potatoes
1 tbsp olive oil
225 g/8 oz baby squid, cleaned and cut into rings
white parts of 2 leeks, chopped
large glass of dry white wine or vermouth
a bunch of fresh dill, chopped
25 g/1 oz butter
25 g/1 oz plain flour
1 bay leaf
grated nutmeg
salt and pepper
12 fat scallops with large corals

Preheat the oven to 180°C/350°F/Gas Mark 4. Put the piece of pollack in a gratin dish with 300 ml/10 fl oz of the milk and a knob of butter, and bake for 15 minutes. Turn the fish into a deeper baking dish, flaking it gently and extracting any bones, but keeping it in largish bits. Reserve the cooking liquid. Boil the potatoes, and mash thoroughly.

While the pollack is cooking, gently heat the oil in a saucepan and cook the squid until barely translucent. Add the leeks and cook for a further 2–3 minutes, then add the wine or vermouth. Bring to simmering point, cover and simmer gently for 10–15 minutes. Throw in a generous amount of chopped dill and take the pan off the heat. Using a slotted spoon, transfer the squid and leeks to the dish with the pollack, reserving the liquid.

Melt the butter in a saucepan, add the flour and cook, stirring, for 1 minute. Add the bay leaf and a good pinch of nutmeg, and gradually stir in the liquid from the pollack to make a béchamel sauce. Remove from the heat and stir in the wine and dill from the squid mixture. Add more milk if you like a heavily sauced pie, but keep the mixture quite thick. Taste and adjust the seasoning, then pour the sauce over the fish.

Prepare the scallops, slicing the white parts into two or three discs, depending on their thickness, and leaving the corals whole unless they are really huge. The secret of this pie is to add the scallops raw to the cooked fish at this point.

Top the pie with mashed potato and cook in the oven for 15–20 minutes, until browned and bubbling on top. The scallops will be just cooked, and exuding their flavour, without having set firmly or breaking up.

Scallop, pollack and squid pie.

OPINEL

Mackerel

I have never thought mackerel benefited from much interference. They are dramatically at their best eaten on the day they are caught; when bought from the fishmonger the texture and flavour are not remotely comparable.

I got used to gutting and washing scores of them a few hours after we'd caught them. I would bake them in the oven at 180°C/350°F/Gas Mark 4, with pepper and butter or olive oil, for 15 minutes, before eating them plain and unadorned, with mashed potato.

The rich oiliness is cut if you roll them in a drop of olive oil, coat them in oatmeal and bake for the same amount of time.

A good fruity salad should follow, perhaps avocado, orange and chicory, tossed in a light dressing with a little of the juice from the oranges. Nothing too oily after mackerel.

Roasted Garlic Mashed Potatoes

The one variation that I think does work with mackerel is to roast a few cloves of garlic – say 2–3 per person – in their skins, coated in some olive oil, in the oven until soft when spiked with a skewer. Pop them out of their skins and mash them with a fork, adding a little olive oil. As you are mashing the potatoes, add a little of the garlicky oil mixture and a drop of milk at a time – and forego any butter. It gives the potatoes a wonderfully pungent, earthy flavour and is particularly good with fish.

Irish hospitality is legendary. Years of famine and deprivation seem to have shaped a caste of mind whereby food, warmth, the sharing of a dish, a drink, is as much a ritual as a handshake. I started 'visiting' as a child, cycling or riding to farms up tracks near the beaches or mountains, or staying with the parents of friends also working at Old Head.

There are some old farmers, brothers and sisters who live at the head of a valley enclosed by mountains, whom I have been visiting for 25 years. The track wending through the valley bottom, streams and waterfalls on either side, seems to go on for ever, the mountains rising starkly, the low hills strewn with boulders as though some great Ice Age catastrophe had thrown them down the mountain, and there they have remained.

The first time I went beyond the house at the end of the track, forded the river and climbed through the bog to the lake nestling in a mountain beyond, the inhabitants of the cottage were there waiting for me on my return. It is event enough for anyone to pass their door. I was greeted by two men and two women, and brought into the kitchen where the hens and a sheepdog tied to a tree stump seemed as at home as the human occupants. Disarmed, as always, by the easy curiosity that is a defining Irish characteristic, I told them where I came from and what I was doing, and was asked to stay for tea. Tea was, and still is, the main event of the day, when everyone has come in from the land. A huge fireplace with the obligatory turf fire, a blackened kettle hanging from a hook, and a flat lidded pan for cooking the huge, hub-cap-sized cakes of soda bread. When the water boiled, one of the women crouched down with tongs and deftly scooped bits of glowing embers, banking them up around the teapot on the hearth. I will never forget the smoky, turf-scented cup of tea (I think the best I have ever tasted), and the bread held against the chest and sliced perilously towards it, on which were thickly spread butter and cold mutton. A feast.

One of the two brothers, Johnny, has since died, but I remember when he and Paddy were still alive, they were prepared to strike a deal. In the days when a girlfriend of mine and I visited from Boathaven, we went in Wendy's car. It was a rust-ridden old Fiat, but Paddy and Johnny seemed to see it differently. Our joint hands were asked in marriage, their argument being that the dowry we brought would get them around, and we, in our turn, wouldn't want for anything! They and their sisters had plenty of sheep, water from the river and, magically, a house

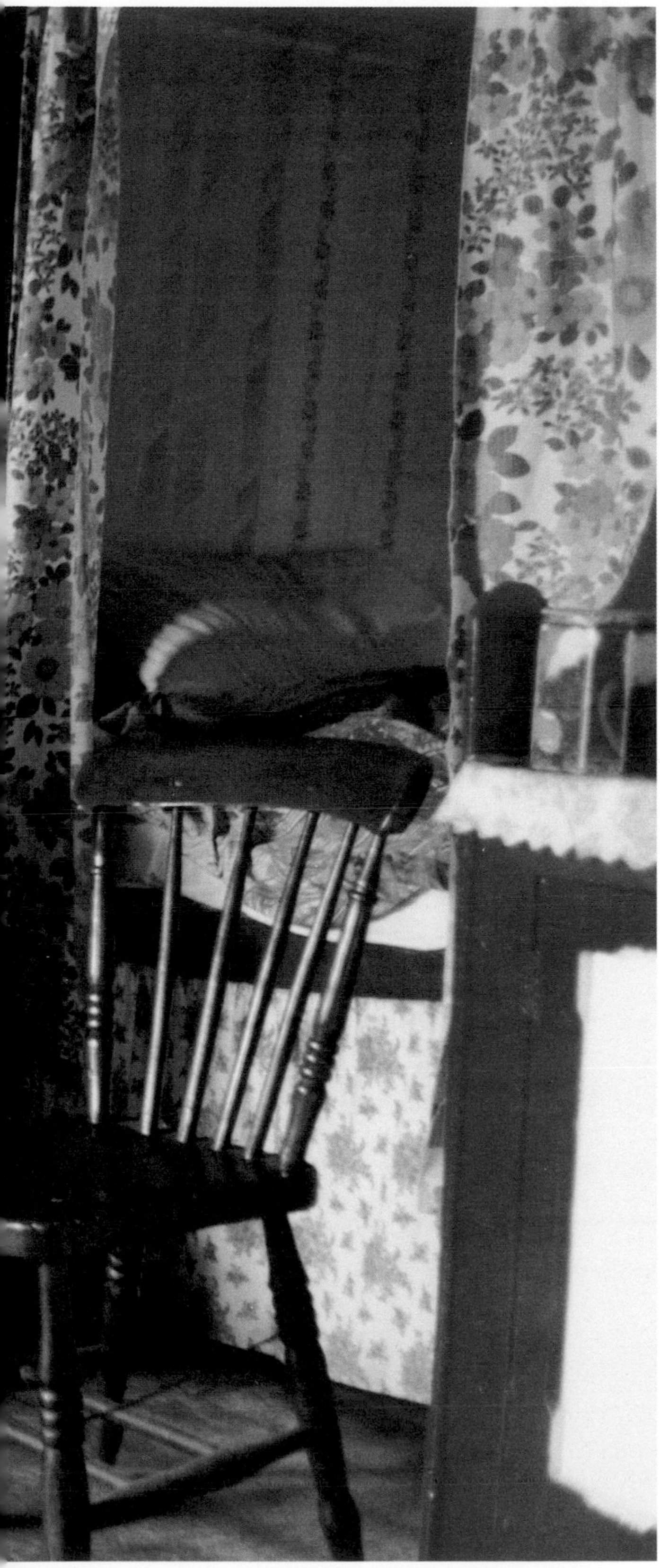

Paddy and his coileach.

unencumbered by any 20th-century technology, plumbing or cookers. The three rooms are the same today. Paddy's bed, a source of total fascination to my children, must be one of Ireland's last remaining *coileachs*. It is a traditional bed built into an alcove in the kitchen, by the fire, with curtains and a quilt, the traditional place for the most senior member of the family to sleep, usually a grandmother or grandfather.

The meat is still salted and kept in barrels in the winter, and Paddy makes his own sugons, twisted strands of straw for thatching the barns. Both sisters, in their eighties now, look after the house, one knitting socks, the younger, less arthritic one helping on the land and with the sheep, and cooking and running the place.

Sometimes when I visit them I take a small bottle of Jameson, or a new pipe for Paddy, and we all sit around the fire and talk of everything from sheep prices to the city. Stew cooked on the fire with everything in one pot and such treats as unfashionably delicious mutton are my favourite kind of food, as good as their ingredients, all the flavours intensified by the long, slow cooking, and, in this case, the added joy of the turf smoke. In the following recipes you can, of course, substitute lamb for mutton, but it is mutton that carries the strong flavours and spices best.

Roast Mutton and Caper Sauce

Serves 8

1.8–2 kg/4–4½ lb shoulder or leg of mutton or lamb
a generous bunch of rosemary
3–4 cloves garlic, sliced
1 tsp ground ginger
1 tsp cloves, crushed
1 tsp salt
40 g/1½ oz plain flour
black pepper
1–2 tbsp olive oil
2–3 onions, sliced
25 g/1 oz butter
1 bay leaf
450 ml/ 15 fl oz milk
grated nutmeg
2 tbsp baby capers, rinsed

Roast mutton makes a wonderful cold dish, in which case you can make the caper sauce separately in a saucepan to ensure a creamy colour and a less fatty sauce.

Preheat the oven to 200–220°C/400–425°F/Gas Mark 6–7. Make slashes through the fat and into the meat of your mutton or lamb, and insert a sprig of rosemary and a slice of garlic into each slash. Mix together the ginger, cloves, salt and 15 g/½ oz of the flour and rub this over the meat. Season with black pepper, dribble some olive oil over the top, and place the joint on a bed of sliced onions in a roasting tin. Roast in the oven; if you like it pink, 1½ hours for a 1.8–2 kg/4–4½ lb joint should be fine, but test by inserting a skewer into a thick part of the meat – the juices should run out tinged pink if it is slightly underdone.

Leave the roast joint on your carving board to rest (and for the juices that have been forced to the centre of the meat to redistribute themselves), under a tight wrapping of foil and a tea towel for about 20 minutes while you make the sauce.

Add the butter to the cooking juices and onions in the roasting tin. Add the remaining 25 g/1 oz of flour and stir it in well, mashing the onion as you go. Add the bay leaf. Heat the milk in a separate saucepan and gradually add the hot milk until thickened and smooth, and then simmer for 20 minutes. A suspicion of nutmeg will help the flavour. Strain the sauce through a sieve, pressing the onions with a wooden spoon to extract all the flavour. Add the capers, and serve alongside the meat and vegetables.

Mutton Braised in Brandy and White Wine

SERVES 8

2 tbsp olive oil
1.8–2 kg/4–4½ lb leg of mutton or lamb
large measure of brandy
2–3 cloves garlic per person
300 ml/10 fl oz dry white wine
3–4 sprigs of thyme

OPTIONAL:
1 fennel bulb, halved, per person

Heat the oil in a heavy-bottomed casserole and gently brown the meat all over. Add the brandy and set light to it with a taper. Wait until it has finished crackling and the flames have died down, then add the garlic and wine. Strew the thyme on top of the joint, cover with greaseproof paper and a tight lid, and simmer very gently for 2–2½ hours.

After 1½ hours, steam the halved fennel bulbs if you are using them until the central cores are just resistant to the point of a knife. Add them to the casserole and turn them in the juices, then replace the lid and simmer for a final 5–10 minutes.

Alternatively, instead of the fennel, serve with flageolet or haricot beans.

Flageolet Beans

SERVES 8
AS AN ACCOMPANIMENT

450 g/1 lb dried flageolet beans
½ an onion, in its skin
2–3 sticks of celery
2–3 carrots, cut into chunks
2–3 leek tops
1 bouquet garni with 2 bay leaves, 2 sprigs of rosemary, thyme and parsley, tied together with string
1–2 tbsp olive oil
2 shallots, finely chopped
3–4 cloves garlic, finely chopped
salt and pepper
OPTIONAL:
½ a lemon
2 tomatoes, skinned, seeded and chopped

Soak the beans in cold water overnight. Drain, rinse, and put them in a large saucepan with water or stock to cover the beans. Add the onion, 1 of the sticks of celery cut into three or four pieces, the carrots, leek tops and bouquet garni. Bring to the boil, skim off the scum, cover tightly, and simmer until the beans are tender, about 1½ hours.

Purée a couple of tablespoons of the beans in a little of the cooking liquid. Remove and discard the other vegetables, and drain the remaining flageolets.

Finely chop the remaining stick of celery, and sauté in the olive oil with the shallots and garlic until softened. Add the whole flageolets and mix gently. Season with salt and pepper. Stir in the bean purée, adding a squeeze of lemon juice and a couple of chopped tomatoes if you like, and serve alongside the lamb.

Flageolet or Haricot Bean Casserole

SERVES 8 AS AN ACCOMPANIMENT; 4–6 AS A LUNCH OR SUPPER DISH

450 g/1 lb flageolet or haricot beans, cooked (see preceding recipe)
a handful of brown bread
a handful of fresh parsley
2–3 tbsp grated Parmesan cheese
25–50 g/1–2 oz butter

OPTIONAL:
2–3 rashers of smoked bacon, cooked and chopped

This makes a wonderful one-pot casserole in its own right. You can add a few rashers of oak-smoked bacon if you like, or keep it vegetarian.

Preheat the oven to 180°C/350°F/Gas Mark 4. Put the bean mixture in a casserole, with the bacon if you are using it, and add a little more of the bean cooking liquid so that the mixture almost fills the dish. Whizz together the brown bread and parsley in a food processor and add the grated Parmesan. Spread this mixture over the beans, dot with butter, and cook in the oven for 20–25 minutes.

Lamb Boulangère

SERVES 4

675 g/1½ lb potatoes, sliced
salt and pepper
2 large onions, thinly sliced
3–4 cloves garlic, sliced
about 300 ml/10 fl oz meat or chicken stock, hot
1–2 tbsp olive oil or butter
4 large or 8 small lamb chops

This is really an upside-down Lancashire hotpot, a deliciously warming casserole.

Preheat the oven to 180°C/350°F/Gas Mark 4. Butter a gratin or slightly deeper dish. Add a layer of potatoes, season them, then add a layer of sliced onions and garlic, another layer of potatoes, and season again. Pour on the hot stock, cover with greaseproof paper and cook in the oven for 1 hour.

Heat the oil or butter in a frying pan and brown the chops on both sides, then lay them on top of the potatoes. Cook for about another 20 minutes.

Serve with a root vegetable, preferably puréed to soak up the juice. Either a carrot and swede purée with butter and nutmeg, or a parsnip purée to which you have added a cooked and puréed eating apple (Cox's have the best flavour).

The coileach and dresser in Paddy's house.

Braised Lamb Shanks with Champ

Serves 4

4 lamb shanks, 8–10 cm/ 3–4 inches long
2 tbsp plain flour
salt and pepper
2–3 tbsp olive oil
4 onions, sliced
6–7 cloves garlic, crushed
2–3 sprigs of rosemary and thyme, finely chopped
300 ml/10 fl oz dry white wine
150 ml/5 fl oz balsamic vinegar

Optional:
2 strips of lemon rind

This is an Italian and Irish combination – the creamy, buttery champ soaking up the piquant juices from the lamb. It is a cheap and extremely hearty dish.

Turn the shanks in the seasoned flour, and shake off any excess flour. Heat the oil in a heavy-bottomed casserole. When hot, add the lamb shanks and brown all over. Remove the meat with a slotted spoon and put to one side. Add the onions, garlic and herbs, and sauté until golden and softened. Raise the heat and add the wine and vinegar together. Bubble them furiously for 2–3 minutes to reduce.

Return the shanks to the casserole and cover with greaseproof paper and a lid. You can add a couple of strips of lemon rind if you like. Lower the heat and simmer very gently for 2 hours. Turn the shanks from time to time, and add more wine if the liquid is evaporating. Longer cooking won't hurt them: the meat should fall off the bone.

Half an hour before you want to eat, start cooking the champ.

Champ

1 kg/2½ lb floury potatoes, such as King Edwards
300 ml/10 fl oz creamy milk
50–85 g/2–3 oz butter
6 spring onions, finely chopped
salt and pepper

Simmer the potatoes until tender. Drain off the water, cover the pan and let them sit for a few minutes. Put the milk and 50 g/2 oz of the butter in a saucepan and heat to boiling point. Add the spring onions, turn off the heat, and let them infuse the milk.

Mash the potatoes, then add the milk, butter and spring onion mixture, stirring until smooth. Season to taste. You can make a well in the centre and add an extra lump of butter to melt into the champ if you like.

Braised lamb shanks.

CHAPTER 2

Return to the West

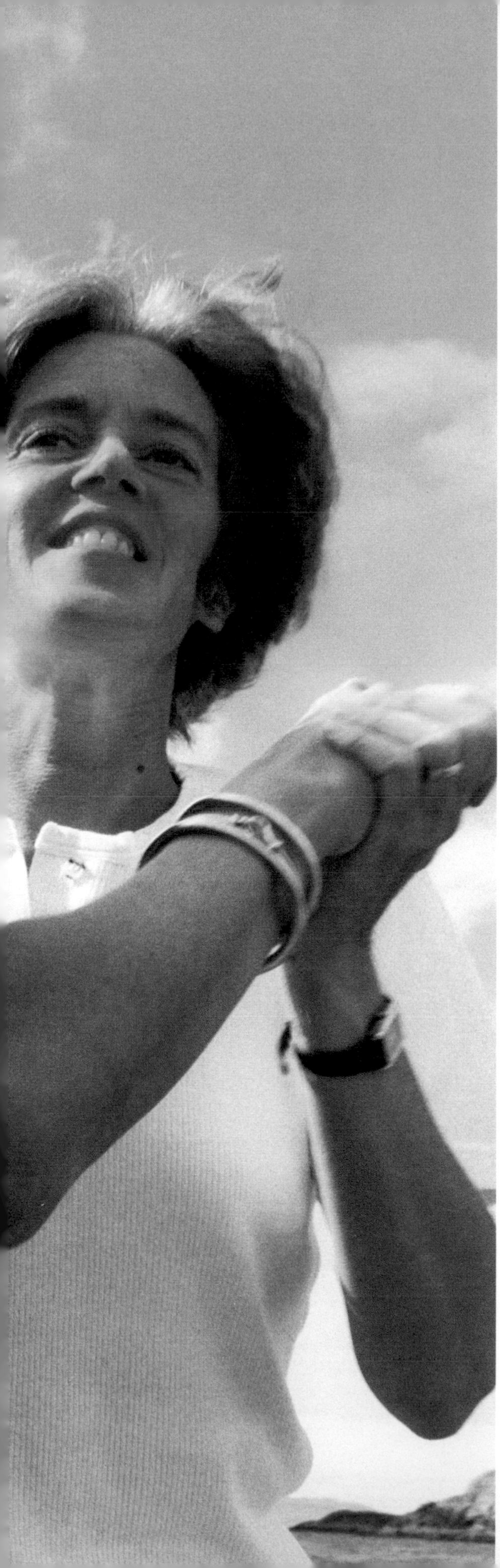

When Alec died, it was the end of another era. There are few people whose doorsteps one can turn up on with a suitcase and stay for the summer. Perhaps, also, in one's twenties, one abandons quite consciously huge swathes of one's childhood past.

When I returned to Ireland seven years ago, it was with my husband and three young children. We rented a friend's cottage up a track in the Sheaffrey Hills, and enjoyed several weeks of calmly brilliant azure sea and skied days, a thing of such rarity that when it happens it is talked about, in disbelieving tones, through winter and summer for years to come.

Pushing a pram across the vast empty beaches, we pitched camp in the dunes and collected huge piles of bleached driftwood for bonfires. At low tide, scores of weedy rock pools appeared, with fleets of shrimps scudding from side to side like missiles. We

Merci and I dancing 'Shoe the Donkey' on board John Kilcoyne's boat.

netted and pailed and netted and pailed until each bucket looked like a civil war in miniature, as the larger, more whiskery, shrimps attacked the little ones. The fire lit, we heated huge tins of sea-water, and plopped the catch in once the water was boiling, watching the shrimps fizz and pinken almost instantly. The children became expert at unfurling the meat from the bendy carapaces, and gently separating it from the tail. The sweet, salty shrimps need nothing else – we never get as far as potting them – at most I take a tub of homemade mayonnaise to dip them into. Very little beats food you have grown, foraged for or fished yourself, cooked and eaten in as short a time as possible.

We met up with my childhood friend Merci Kilcoyne, and her husband John, and spent some wonderful days on his boat, hauling mussels in off the ropes they grow on, grading them on deck, and cooking them on a little Primus as we chugged up the Killary towards the open sea. Seals were strewn along the rocks, and slipped gracefully into the water as we passed them, and further out at the mouth of the bay the dolphins jumped in arcs of perfect synchronicity, two by two – or sometimes three.

We stopped off on the northern shore and clambered up to Derry village, deserted since famine times, and now an eerily empty place of tumbledown stone ruins and patches where the grass has still not entirely hidden the corrugated mounds and furrows of what were once potato plots for whole families. But for the sheep and a few wild goats, it is a penetratingly quiet place. You can look out over the massively deep fjord of the Killary, across to the southern side where the ruins of a walled track built along the hillside during the famine climb erratically up and down the rocky slopes, hiding perhaps five or six ruined houses, otherwise an unpopulated landscape.

Picnics can be as dull as they can be inventive and wonderful. The vagaries of the weather aside, it seems to me that the things that usually taste best are those that are warm, rather than those that you have struggled to keep hot or cold, and things that have an even chance of staying fresh and preserving their texture. Soggy sandwiches and crumbling slices of railway cake are about as appetizing as over-hard-boiled eggs and greasy, inferior sausages. Unless it is for *pan bagna*, I never put the fillings in the bread until people are ready for lunch. There are plenty of delicious things like *polpettone* (Italian meat loaf), homity pies, chicken in barbecue sauce and *pissaladières* that travel well and can be made before you take off for the day. The same is true of soups, salads and shallow-dished fruit pies. At least one of the following should tempt the palate of the most jaded and cynical of picnickers. For a picnic, I always take a selection of these dishes, but each makes a perfect lunch in its own right, with just a salad as accompaniment.

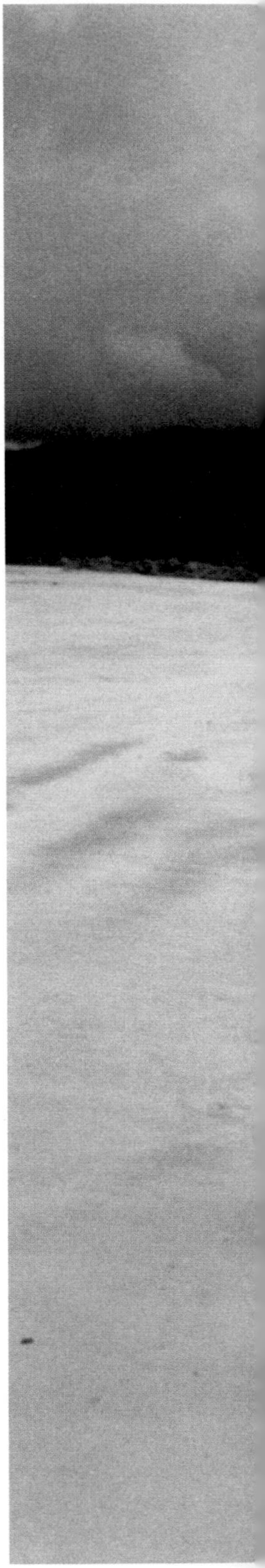

Charissa's friends, Charlene and Stephanie, on the beach.

Italian Meat Loaf

Serves 8–10 for a picnic;
4–6 as a lunch dish

450 g/1 lb each of minced veal and pork (good lean meat)
4 eggs, beaten
2 cloves garlic, finely chopped
1 onion, finely chopped
2 tbsp chopped fresh flat-leaf parsley
salt and pepper
2 plum tomatoes, sliced
2 eggs, boiled for 6 minutes and sliced
175–200 g/6–7 oz lean smoked bacon, cooked, or ham chopped
25 g/1 oz each Parmesan and Gruyère cheese, grated

Preheat the oven to 150°C/300°F/Gas Mark 2. In a large mixing bowl, mix together the minced meat, beaten eggs, garlic, onion, parsley, salt and pepper.

Oil a heavy-bottomed 30 x 10 x 10 cm/12 x 4 x 4 inch lidded loaf tin and put half the mixture into it, pressing it down firmly. Add a layer of tomatoes, then a layer of the sliced boiled eggs and chopped bacon or ham, and sprinkle the grated cheeses on top. Cover with the rest of the meat mixture. Put a piece of greaseproof paper under the lid, and cook in the oven for 1½ hours. You can remove the paper and lid for the last 30 minutes to brown the top.

Leave to cool to room temperature or completely cold. Take on your picnic as it is, or sliced but kept in shape inside a wrapping of greaseproof paper and foil.

Tricolour Omelette

SERVES 8–10 FOR A PICNIC;
4–6 AS A LUNCH DISH

about 5 tbsp olive oil
1 tsp fresh thyme leaves
450 g/1 lb plum tomatoes, skinned, seeded and chopped
450 g/1 lb small, tender spinach leaves
2 cloves garlic, peeled but left whole
9 eggs
100 ml/3½ fl oz double cream
grated nutmeg
salt and pepper
25 g/1 oz Parmesan cheese, grated
25 g/1 oz Gruyère cheese, grated

A delicious dish, the red, green and yellow layers setting to a firm creaminess.

Preheat the oven to 150°C/300°F/Gas Mark 2. Heat 2 tablespoons of the oil in a small frying pan with the thyme leaves. Add the tomatoes and sauté briefly, then put on a plate to cool. Drain away any excess liquid.

Heat 3 tablespoons of the oil in a large saucepan and add the spinach leaves and garlic. Cook until softened, and most of the moisture has evaporated. Remove the garlic, chop the spinach, and leave to cool on a plate. Drain away any excess liquid, otherwise it will make the finished dish watery.

Break 3 eggs each into three bowls. To one, add the spinach, 3 tablespoons of the cream, a suspicion of nutmeg, salt and pepper, and whisk together. To the second, add the tomatoes, 2 tablespoons of the cream, salt and pepper, and whisk. To the third, add the grated cheeses, the remaining cream, salt and pepper, and whisk.

Oil a heavy-bottomed 30 x 10 x 10 cm/12 x 4 x 4 inch loaf tin. Pour in the tomato mixture. Stand the tin in a deep roasting tin with boiling water coming halfway up its sides, and cook in the oven for 20 minutes. It should be just set: not firm, but not runny. If the centre is runny, leave it a bit longer, or the layers will run together. Pour in the cheese layer and cook for a further 20 minutes. Again, it should be just set, so check carefully. Finally pour in the spinach layer and cook for 20 minutes or until set.

Leave to cool down considerably. You can either turn it out and take it wrapped in greaseproof paper and foil to your picnic, or slice it in thick wedges straight from the tin when you are ready to eat it.

My son I larry on board John Kilcoyne's boat.

Chicken in a Fruity Barbecue Sauce

Serves 6

125 g/4 oz tomato ketchup
1 tbsp Japanese shoyu sauce or dark soy sauce
1 tbsp Worcestershire sauce
2 tsp cider vinegar
1 tbsp olive oil
2 tsp tomato purée or 1 tsp harissa
2 tsp grainy mustard
1 tbsp clear honey
2 tsp molasses sugar
juice of 1 small orange
3 cloves garlic, crushed
2.5 cm/1 inch square piece of fresh ginger, chopped and squeezed through a garlic press
salt and pepper
up to 12 pieces of chicken

Use chicken legs, thighs or drumsticks. If using the smaller pieces, allow 2 per person or greedy child. I have never known even the fussiest of children to turn up their noses at this dish, even if they purport to hate ginger or any of the stronger ingredients. If you are cooking for grown-ups and feel like something hotter, add 1 teaspoon of harissa instead of the tomato purée.

Mix together all the ingredients except for the chicken. Put the chicken in this mixture and marinate for at least 3 hours, turning when you remember. (You can leave it overnight if you want.)

Preheat the oven to 180°C/350°F/Gas Mark 4. Put the chicken and marinade in a roasting tin and cover with foil. Bake for about 30 minutes. Test by inserting a skewer into the meat: if the juice runs nearly clear, the chicken is almost cooked. Remove the foil for the final 5–10 minutes. Once the foil is off, the sauce will reduce and adhere to the meat.

Leave to cool, then put the chicken in an airtight container. If there is a lot of sauce left, put it in a separate bowl to take on your picnic. This dish is delicious hot, so, if you get rained off, or feel like cooking it on a grill over the fire, or on a barbecue, don't hesitate. Just cook the sauce separately by heating it through in a little saucepan.

Homity Pies

Makes 6

Shortcrust Pastry (see page 158), made with 225 g/8 oz wholemeal flour (organic if possible)
325 g/12 oz potatoes
25 g/1 oz butter
3–4 tbsp milk or cream
450 g/1 lb onions, finely chopped
3 tbsp olive oil
2 cloves garlic, crushed
2 tbsp chopped fresh parsley (or mixed herbs: parsley, chives, thyme)
125 g/4 oz strong Cheddar cheese, grated
salt and pepper
2 ripe tomatoes, sliced

Preheat the oven to 220°C/425°F/Gas Mark 7. Roll out the pastry thinly and use to line six individual tart tins, 10 cm/4 inches in diameter. If you don't have them, make one larger tart in a 30 cm/12 inch diameter tin. Chill for at least 20 minutes. Bake the pastry blind for 5 minutes (10 minutes if you are making one large tart). Remove the greaseproof paper and beans and return the pastry to the oven for 5 minutes.

Meanwhile, boil the potatoes until soft, drain and mash them with the butter and milk or cream. Sauté the onions in the oil until golden and softened. Stir into the potato mixture with the garlic, herbs, half the cheese, and the seasoning. Leave to cool.

Fill the pastry cases with the mixture, sprinkle with the remaining cheese and a slice of tomato, and bake in the oven for 20 minutes, until gratinéd and golden on top. Leave to cool slightly and wrap in foil to eat warm, or leave to cool completely.

Cracked Wheat Salad

Serves 8–10 for a picnic; 4–6 as a lunch dish

450 g/1 lb bulgar wheat
1 small onion, finely chopped
1 clove garlic, finely chopped
salt and pepper
a handful of fresh parsley, and/or fresh mint, finely chopped
a handful of fresh coriander, finely chopped, if not using mint
6 tbsp olive oil
6 tbsp lemon juice

Soak the bulgar wheat in cold water until it has swollen and expanded enormously; this should take about 30 minutes. Drain in a sieve, pressing down firmly, then squeeze out any excess moisture by hand. Mix in the chopped onion and garlic. Season, then add the herbs, olive oil and lemon juice. Taste – it should be very lemony and not too oily.

If you like, add some or all of the following: skinned, seeded, chopped tomatoes; roasted red peppers, skinned and seeded; skinned chopped cucumber; crumbled feta or goats' cheese; black garlicky olives. Pile on to a serving dish and surround with lettuce leaves.

Marinated Mackerel with Potato Salad

SERVES 6–8

6–8 mackerel fillets, all bones and skin removed

MARINADE:
125 ml/4 fl oz olive oil
125 ml/4 fl oz dry white wine
50 ml/2 fl oz white wine vinegar
125 ml/4 fl oz water
2 tbsp Pernod
1 lemon, sliced
1 bay leaf
a few sprigs of parsley, dill and thyme
1 carrot, finely sliced
1 stick of celery, finely chopped
1 shallot, finely sliced
a generous pinch of molasses sugar
salt and pepper

POTATO SALAD:
450 g/1 lb Jersey or Pink Fir Apple potatoes
1 shallot, finely chopped
4 tbsp olive oil
1 tbsp white wine vinegar
2 tbsp finely chopped fresh parsley
salt and pepper

Not quite a tartare, but a delicious way of 'pickling' the fish without cooking it.

Cut the mackerel into long, thin strips, about 8 cm/3 inches long and 1 cm/½ inch wide. Put all the marinade ingredients together in a bowl and add the fish, making sure it is submerged. Cover with cling film and refrigerate for at least 18 hours.

A couple of hours before you want to eat, prepare the potato salad. Boil the potatoes and slice them while warm. Mix them with the chopped shallot, olive oil, vinegar, parsley and salt and pepper to taste.

Put a layer of potato salad on each individual plate, and a fillet of mackerel with its vegetables and herbs on top.

Marinated mackerel. They can be marinated cut into strips and skinned.

Red onion pissaladière.

Red Onion Pissaladière

SERVES 8–10 FOR A PICNIC;
4–6 AS A LUNCH DISH

50 g/2 oz butter
200 g/7 oz wholemeal or plain flour
salt
½ oz/15 g fresh yeast
1 egg

FILLING:
450 g/1 lb red onions, very finely sliced
3 tbsp olive oil
3–4 tomatoes, skinned, seeded and chopped
4 cloves garlic, chopped
sprig of thyme
salt and pepper
small tin of anchovies, drained

This is glorious picnic food, with a pungent, sweet onion and anchovy filling; it is best served warm.

Cut the butter into small pieces and rub it into the flour. Add a pinch of salt. Dissolve the yeast in 2 tablespoons of tepid water. Make a well in the centre of the flour and add the egg and yeast. Mix it all together and knead the mixture until it no longer sticks to the bowl. Put the mixture on a cloth in a warm place and leave it to rise for a couple of hours.

Pre-heat the oven to 200°C/400°F/Gas Mark 6. Stew the onions very gently in the olive oil in a covered saucepan. They are ready when they are totally wilted and golden, after about 30 minutes. Add the tomatoes, half the garlic, and the leaves from the thyme. Season with salt and pepper and simmer until the mixture is quite thick. Pound the drained anchovies together with the remaining garlic and stir this into the mixture when you have taken it off the heat.

Sprinkle the dough with flour and knock it back, then knead it into a ball again. Press it into a well-oiled flan tin, working from the middle outwards until it rises up round the sides. Spread the filling over the dough and place the flan tin on a baking sheet in the oven for 20 minutes. Reduce the heat to 180°C/350°F/Gas Mark 4 and cook for another 20 minutes.

Dolmades Made with Cabbage Leaves

SERVES 8–10 FOR A PICNIC;
4–6 AS A LUNCH DISH

125 g/4 oz long-grain brown rice
3–4 tbsp olive oil
1 small onion, finely chopped
3 cloves garlic, finely chopped
½ tsp ground cumin
225 g/8 oz minced lamb
1 tbsp tomato purée
1 tomato, skinned, seeded and chopped
150 ml/5 fl oz red wine
300–450 ml/½–¾ pint chicken stock
1 head of green cabbage
salt and pepper
3 tbsp finely chopped fresh parsley
1 tbsp finely chopped fresh mint
a handful of pine nuts
a handful of raisins

Boil the rice until just tender, drain and set aside. Heat 2 tablespoons of the oil in a saucepan and gently sauté the onion and garlic until softened but not brown. Add the cumin, then the minced lamb, tomato purée and chopped tomato. Add the red wine and bring to boiling point. Add 300 ml/10–15 fl oz of the stock, again bring to boiling point, then cover and simmer very gently for about 1 hour.

While the mixture is simmering, blanch the leaves of the cabbage in boiling water until softened – a few minutes should do it. Refresh under cold water and drain well.

Preheat the oven to 180°C/350°F/Gas Mark 4. Add more stock to the lamb mixture if it looks dry. Season with salt and pepper, add the herbs, pine nuts and raisins, then the rice, and mix well together. Lay out the cabbage leaves and place a tablespoon of the rice mixture on each leaf. Start rolling up the leaf, and after you have rolled the mixture over through 360 degrees, fold both sides of the leaf in towards the middle, then carry on rolling. Pack the little parcels tightly into a roasting dish greased with olive oil. Add some hot stock, and a little red wine if you like, to come halfway up the parcels. Bake in the oven for 30–45 minutes. If the liquid is getting absorbed quickly and the parcels appear to be drying out, add more stock and wine, and cover with a sheet of greaseproof paper until cooked.

Dolmades made with cabbage leaves.

Spiced apple pie.

Spiced Apple Pie

SERVES 6

Shortcrust Pastry (see page 158), made with 325 g/12 oz flour – I usually use wholewheat flour
50 g/2 oz light muscovado sugar
50 g/2 oz dark molasses sugar
¼ tsp ground cloves
¼ tsp ground cinnamon
⅛ tsp grated nutmeg
1 tbsp plain flour
grated rind and juice of ½ a lemon
grated rind and juice of ½ an orange
675 g/1½ lb Cox's apples, peeled and sliced
25–50 g/1–2 oz butter
1 small egg, beaten

OPTIONAL:
granulated sugar for the top

Preheat the oven to 200°C/400°F/Gas Mark 6. Roll out half the pastry and use to line a greased large pie dish – the Irish usually use a shallow pie plate.

Combine the sugars, spices, flour and grated rinds and strew a little of the mixture on the pastry base. Cover with some of the sliced apples and some more of the sugar mixture. Repeat until the dish is densely filled. Add the lemon and orange juices and knobs of butter. Roll out the remaining pastry to make the top crust. Crimp and flute the pastry edges together with a fork. Decorate with an apple made from the pastry trimmings and make one or two slits in the top crust to let out the steam. Brush lightly with beaten egg. Bake in the oven for 35–40 minutes. Leave to cool slightly, then strew granulated sugar over the top of the warm pie if you wish. Wrap in foil if you are taking it on a picnic.

Rhubarb, Orange and Honey Pie

SERVES 6

Cut 675 g/1½ lb of rhubarb into 1 cm/½ inch chunks and stew in the juice of ½ an orange until tender. If the stewed rhubarb is very liquid, decant some of the juice for pouring over the pie when cooked. Sweeten the rhubarb to taste with half muscovado sugar and half clear honey. Add the grated rind of 1 orange. Put the mixture on the pastry base, dot with butter, and add the top pastry crust. Bake as above.

Serve warm, with a jug of single cream and a jug of the rhubarb juice, sweetened to taste. Or wrap the pie in foil to take to the beach!

CHAPTER 3

My House in Mayo

The second year we decamped to the west of Ireland for the summer I realized my maddest dream. It was one of those days when the bog mist never rises, but finally gives way to something squally and unrelentingly wet. We had half-heartedly decided to drive along the coast and walk the headland, and were meandering along the track that finally pours and switchbacks itself to its end on the beach, when, through the murk, I saw on my left a 'For Sale' sign. I couldn't really see the house as by then the wind was gusting straight off the Atlantic, and the rain was coming down in stair-rods. From the top of the track by the squat, single-storey stone and slate house, I could see nothing of the view; the rain and the clouds were interchangeable. I decided there and then to buy it. I hadn't even crossed the threshold,

My house in Mayo.

but I knew exactly what the house looked out on to: the bog behind, from which the mountain reared, dominating one skyline, and, to the fore, miles of beach, sea, and the last islands before America.

The walk abandoned, I headed straight for the estate agent, 25 miles away, and then back to confirm my decision. Surrounded by two acres, and with turbary rights (to cut the turf from the bog behind), it didn't seem to matter what the inside of the house was like.

I had vowed since childhood to have a house on that particular stretch of coast one day, but how many other things does one determine to do, only to look back and wonder why one ever wanted them so passionately? Three days later I put in my first offer, knowing that we were leaving for England that weekend. I think the bemused solicitor did his best to draw my attention to the wildness of the winters, and the need for a thorough survey, but when I pointed out that I had wintered and Christmased with Alec at Old Head, and that the best local surveyor had been a friend since childhood, he knew he could do no more. That was that. Back to England to try to raise the money before Christmas.

I decided to go back in the late autumn with Alan, an old friend who is a wonderful Somerset builder, and see if he could be persuaded to fall in love with the place and do it up. The plan was to move in by the following summer, the summer of '92. Alan and I found ourselves surveying the not exactly culinarily kosher combination of mushrooms and salt. The bath, rooted almost in the earth floor, was blooming black fungus, and the salt, whipped straight off the sea, interpenetrated everything, standing out from the walls in long shards of crystal. The flat-roofed patched extension was not putting up much of a fight to keep out water, and my insurers had already said a pitched slate roof would have to be built into the main one before they would agree to take the place on. The old fireplaces needed digging out, there was wiring, plumbing and heating to do, doors, window frames and floors to replace, a kitchen and porch to put in and – as we were to find out later – a new septic tank. Luckily, Alan took one look at the view and decided it was worth staying for, and so began the first of many trips, which he now does with his wife Chris. The first time he brought her out in their caravan, the house was totally uninhabitable, with the floor a network of Venetian canals dug out for the pipes, and no cons, ancient or modern. One night the wind was so strong Alan had to weight the caravan down with lumps of concrete to stop it taking off. Somehow he got the new roof on in a Bahamic ten days in

January, working by lamp from before dawn until well past dark. On the eleventh day the storms came, but by then the hatches were battened down and the last slate hung.

That summer I moved in – with a Primus for a cooker; squatting down (attired in T-shirt and knickers) to wash up in a bowl in the yard, looking out on to the mountain – was unsurpassable.

Some neighbours I knew already, others, mostly local sheep farmers, immediately arrived with children and presents. Eggs from the hens, homemade porter cake, freshly churned butter, milk, sacks of turf and, in one case, a kitchen clock!

Returning the hospitality proved tricky for the first two weeks without a cooker or a sink. There is an unspoken rule that doesn't allow anyone to visit in the west of Ireland for longer than ten minutes without being offered food or drink. We had Jameson and water from the stream behind the house, and I seem to remember living off a huge gammon joint from my organic butchers, Swaddles Green in Somerset, that I'd brought out in a cold box.

Gradually order emerged from the chaos, and I could start inviting people back for tea, drinks and supper. A glut of wild salmon from the local rivers selling at £1.99 a pound meant one ate or served little else during the July weeks. The result was that my children believe that the only real fishcake is a salmon one, and that I pretty quickly gave up poaching or cooking them *en papillote*, and tried to give guests something more exciting, such as George Perry-Smith's glorious salmon *en croûte* with ginger and currants (see page 77), or Russian salmon *kulebiaka* (from Jane Grigson's *The Mushroom Feast*).

I discovered a close neighbour was an accordion player by night and a fisherman by day, catching lobsters and crabs. There is a curious local tendency to throw the body of the crab back into the sea, losing the delicate, velvety ochre meat. I begged Seamus to keep the crab intact, and set about making souffléd crab tarts, crabcakes, crab soufflés, pancakes and anything else I could dream up.

The field to the back of the house appeared to have two stunted apple trees bent double and almost horizontal by the wind. The only other edible thing I could find on the land, half-hidden in a tangle of nettles, was some sturdy little blackcurrant canes. These got stripped the moment they dripped ripened from their branches, and turned, via a raw purée, into rich ice creams, mousses and crumble tarts, or, in the case of the blackcurrant leaves, into the subtlest scented sorbet I know.

OVERLEAF: *Cows in a Mayo field.*

Souffléd Crab Tart

This is one of those dishes that makes people gasp with pleasure, first when they see it emerge from the oven perfectly risen, and again when they taste the strong, clear flavour of crab, backed up by Parmesan, Gruyère and a touch of cayenne. A perfect starter, or a main course for lunch or dinner.

SERVES 6

Shortcrust Pastry (see page 158)
450 g/1 lb crab meat, brown and white
salt and pepper
pinch of cayenne pepper
3 eggs, separated
1 tbsp grated Parmesan cheese
1 tbsp grated Gruyère cheese
250 ml/8 fl oz double cream
2 tsp French mustard

Roll out the pastry and use to line a greased 22 cm/9 inch tart tin with a removable base. Chill in the fridge for at least 30 minutes.

Preheat the oven to 200°C/400°F/Gas Mark 6. Bake the pastry blind for 10 minutes, then remove from the oven and turn the oven down to 190°C/375°F/Gas Mark 5. Remove the greaseproof paper and beans.

Season the crab meat with salt, pepper and cayenne, and beat in 1 whole egg and 2 yolks, and then the cheeses, cream and mustard. Whisk the 2 egg whites until stiff, and fold gently and quickly into the crab mixture. Put the mixture into the slightly cooled pastry case and cook in the oven for about 40 minutes, but check after 30 minutes. It will puff up, and should have a slightly 'sad' centre', like a soufflé. I like to serve this with Braised Fennel and Saffron Potatoes.

Braised Fennel

Allow 1 bulb of fennel per person. Trim off the tough outer layer and cut each bulb in half. Steam until just resistant to the point of a knife. Drain and place in a gratin dish, cut-side down. Drizzle with olive oil, pepper and grated Parmesan and put under a hot grill until the cheese has thoroughly melted.

Saffron Potatoes

Allow 675 g/1½ lb Jersey new potatoes in their skins for four people. Sweat them in 25 g/1 oz of butter in a heavy-bottomed casserole for a couple of minutes. Add a good pinch of saffron threads, a bay leaf and a sprig of thyme and shake the pan. Add 125 ml/4 fl oz of hot chicken stock, cover the pan and simmer gently for about 15 minutes. Remove the lid and boil to reduce the liquid until it is a syrupy glaze. Remove the thyme and the bay leaf, add a finely chopped spring onion and another knob of butter if you like, and give them a couple of minutes more.

Ingredients for souffléd crab tart.

Crab Soufflé with a Cucumber and Avocado Sambal

Serves 4

1 tbsp butter
2–3 tbsp day-old brown breadcrumbs
1 tbsp grated Parmesan cheese
pinch of cayenne pepper
1 small tsp curry powder (optional)
325 g/12 oz crab meat, brown and white
1 tsp French mustard
a few drops of Tabasco sauce
2 tsp dry sherry
salt and pepper
150 ml/5 fl oz béchamel Sauce (see below)
1–2 tbsp double cream
3 egg yolks
4 egg whites

Béchamel Sauce:

2 tsp butter
2 tsp plain flour
1 small bay leaf
150 ml/5 fl oz milk
salt and pepper

Soufflés are easy. Timing is all, but that is as much about having people sitting round the table in anticipation as it is about knowing when the soufflé is cooked. This is one of my two favourite soufflé recipes. The other is a Fennel Soufflé (see opposite) which is subtler and quieter somehow, but deliciously unusual. The basic mixture can be prepared in advance, so that you need only 10 minutes' preparation just before cooking the soufflé.

Preheat the oven to 180–190°C/350–375°F/Gas Mark 4–5. First make the béchamel sauce: melt the butter in a saucepan, add the flour and cook, stirring, for 1 minute. Add the bay leaf and gradually stir in the milk. Cook, stirring constantly, until the sauce is thick and smooth. Season to taste.

Butter a soufflé dish generously, then roll the breadcrumbs and half the Parmesan around the inside of the dish, tipping out and reserving what doesn't adhere to the butter. Melt a knob of butter in a saucepan, add the cayenne and curry powder if you are using it, and cook for 1 minute. Remove from the heat and add the crab meat, mustard, Tabasco, sherry and salt and pepper to taste. Warm gently, then stir in the béchamel sauce and the cream. Remove from the heat and stir in the egg yolks. (The mixture can be prepared ahead up to this point.)

Whisk the egg whites until stiff, then cut and fold them briskly and lightly into the mixture. Turn the mixture into the soufflé dish. Sprinkle the remaining Parmesan and breadcrumbs over the top. Fix a piece of greaseproof paper (the top 5 cm/2 inches buttered well on the inside) around the dish, fastening it with a paper clip – when the soufflé has risen and the paper is taken away, this looks spectacular. Bake in the oven for 20–25 minutes: the soufflé should be firm and well risen, with the barest hint of a shudder at the middle if you shake it gently. Bring it directly to the table as soon as you have taken off the greaseproof paper.

Cucumber and Avocado Sambal

½ a cucumber, skinned and seeded
1 red pepper, skinned and seeded
1 avocado
lemon juice, olive oil and balsamic vinegar, to taste
1 tbsp finely chopped fresh dill

While the soufflé is cooking, chop the cucumber as finely as you can – about 3 mm/⅛ inch square. Do the same with the red pepper, and chop the avocado into slightly bigger cubes. Sprinkle on some lemon juice, then a little olive oil and balsamic vinegar, some black pepper and finely chopped dill. This can be served in a separate bowl and provides a good crunchy texture and colour contrast to the soufflé; a scant tablespoon per person is enough.

Fennel Soufflé

SERVES 4

Steam 4–5 halved fennel bulbs, the tough outer skins removed, until tender. Purée thoroughly in a liquidizer or food processor, then leave to cool. If the resulting purée looks watery, cook it down a bit further in a saucepan, or, if possible, spoon off the excess liquid.

Follow the method for the Crab Soufflé (opposite), but cut out the spicy ingredients – so no Tabasco, curry powder, sherry, cayenne or mustard. Instead, add 1 tablespoon each of grated Gruyère and Parmesan cheese when you mix the fennel purée with the béchamel sauce, cream and egg yolks. You can also add some finely chopped parsley and dill to the mixture that coats the dish and the soufflé top. Serve with a spoonful of sambal, as in the preceding recipe.

Crabcakes with Herb Mayonnaise

SERVES 4, ALLOWING 2 CRABCAKES EACH

3–4 tbsp milk
2 thin slices of wholemeal bread, crusts removed
450 g/1 lb crab meat, brown and white
1 large tbsp mayonnaise (preferably homemade)
small pinch of cayenne pepper or harissa
¼ tsp dry English mustard
¼ tsp celery salt
1 tbsp chopped fresh flat-leaf parsley or coriander
½ tsp Worcestershire sauce
salt and pepper
1 egg, beaten
olive oil, for shallow frying

HERB MAYONNAISE:
2 egg yolks
1 tsp French mustard
175–250 ml/6–8 fl oz cold-pressed safflower or sunflower oil
50 ml/2 fl oz cold-pressed olive oil
1 tbsp chopped mixed fresh herbs (for example, lovage, chervil, dill)
½ a lemon
salt and pepper

In Britain we tend to make fishcakes with potato to bind them. The Americans often use bread soaked in milk, as one does for taramasalata, and the result is a light-textured but scrumptiously spicy, crisp crabcake.

Pour the milk over the bread, let it soak in, then squeeze out the bread until it is moderately dry. Put it in a bowl and mash it with a fork. Add all the remaining ingredients except the egg, mix well and season to taste. Add the beaten egg, then shape the mixture into eight cakes, working quickly and lightly. Heat the oil in a large frying pan, drop in the crabcakes and cook until crisp, about 3 minutes on each side.

To make the mayonnaise, stir the egg yolks and mustard together to start emulsification. Then gradually stir in the safflower or sunflower oil, drop by drop to begin with, then in a thin stream. Stir in the olive oil, and when it is thick and like a golden ointment, add the herbs and squeeze in the lemon juice to taste; season with salt and pepper.

Serve with a plain green salad, and crunchy, garlicky Roasted Rosemary Potatoes.

ROASTED ROSEMARY POTATOES

Chop 4 large King Edward or good roasting potatoes into 1 cm/½ inch squares, keeping their skins on. Warm a couple of tablespoons of olive oil on a baking sheet in a hot oven, 200°C/400°F/Gas Mark 6, for a few minutes. Add the potatoes and 7–8 unpeeled cloves of garlic, and strew with a few branches of rosemary. Cook in the oven for about 50 minutes, turning every 15 minutes or so and seasoning with salt and pepper towards the end. I pop the garlic out of its skin and eat it – not everyone is that addicted.

After years of making ice creams by hand, and endlessly taking them out of the freezer and whisking them furiously to stop crystals forming, I have now got the Rolls-Royce of ice cream makers. Yes, I can cut the freezing process dramatically, but a really good ice cream is only as good as its ingredients and how well you've made it in the first place.

The first time I ever made blackcurrant ice cream – or any ice cream – I was 13, at boarding school, and desperate to inject a soupçon of originality into the end-of-term dorm feast. I emptied a large quantity of Ribena into an ice tray, stirred in the cream and a squeeze of lemon, and surreptitiously passed it to the school chef through the kitchen window to freeze. It was delicious. After cold baked beans and sweetcorn (both eaten from the tin), Ritz biscuits and Primula cheese, and the rather more upmarket offerings from one of my grandmother's Fortnum & Mason hampers, which used to arrive erratically but always at an opportune moment, we lay on the floor spooning the ice cream out of the tray, or dipping into it with chocolate Bath Oliver biscuits.

The blackcurrant ice cream I make now, when I've stripped the currants off the branches in Ireland, captures the illicitly delicious richness of the original. Based on vanilla ice cream, it has the raw, gutsy flavour of the uncooked fruit.

Vanilla Ice Cream

SERVES 6 IF THE ONLY PUDDING; UP TO 10 IF ACCOMPANYING ANOTHER PUDDING

1 vanilla pod
300 ml/10 fl oz single cream
4 egg yolks, beaten
vanilla caster sugar (sugar that has been stored with a vanilla pod), to taste
300 ml/10 fl oz double cream, unpasteurized organic if possible

Everyone else removes the vanilla pod at the last moment or sieves the grainy bits out if they've cooked them in. I make no apologies for doing neither. I scoop the seeds out of the pod, cook them in the cream and, even if the ice cream is remaining vanilla, leave them in, making the rich cream colouring speckledy.

Scoop out the seeds from the vanilla pod by cutting all along the pod with a knife, firmly inserting a teaspoon and pulling it along the length of the pod. Put the contents of the spoon into a saucepan with the single cream, and bring just to boiling point. Remove from the heat and leave to infuse for 10–15 minutes. Pour the mixture on to the egg yolks, whisk together, and return to the pan. Stir gently, or whisk, over a low heat, until the mixture has thickened perceptibly and coats a spoon. Do not try and hurry this by turning up the heat, as the mixture will curdle.

Sweeten to taste with vanilla sugar and leave to cool. Whisk the double cream until stiff, pour in the vanilla mixture and fold in gently and thoroughly. Freeze the vanilla mixture or add your choice of flavouring before freezing.

Raw Blackcurrant Ice Cream

SERVES 6–8

The flavour of raw blackcurrants is incomparable in cold puddings.

Swirl 450 g/1 lb raw blackcurrants in a liquidizer or food processor until well puréed, then rub them through a nylon sieve. Add light muscovado sugar to taste, and then a good squeeze from ½ a lemon. Add this to the Vanilla Ice Cream mixture in the preceding recipe, made with a fraction less sugar. Freeze.

Raw Blackcurrant Fool

SERVES 6–8

Follow the method for Raw Blackcurrant Ice Cream, but instead of freezing, spoon the mixture into individual glasses or one big bowl and put it in the fridge for at least 6 hours. You can decorate it with a few blackcurrants and small young mint leaves.

Raw Blackcurrant Mousse

SERVES 6–8

To the raw blackcurrant purée, add 3 egg yolks, then gently beat in 300 ml/10 fl oz of whipped, but not stiff, double cream. Dissolve a packet of gelatine (or the equivalent in leaf gelatine) according to the instructions, and stir well into the mixture. Whisk 4 egg whites until stiff and fold briskly but lightly into the mixture. This is a deliciously light yet intensely flavoured pudding.

Blackcurrant Leaf Sorbet

Serves 6–8

225 g/8 oz caster sugar
600 ml/1 pint water
3 good handfuls of small blackcurrant leaves (not the big, tough ones)
grated rind and juice of 1 lemon
2 egg whites

Herbalists have believed in the power of raspberry leaves and blackcurrant leaves for centuries, particularly during pregnancy – they have properties that are believed to protect against miscarriage – and ruminants eat them if they can get them when in calf. Most importantly, the flavour is unlike any you will ever have experienced, a real new taste, unguessable and unexpected.

Place the sugar and water in a saucepan, heat gently until dissolved, then boil for 10 minutes. Add the blackcurrant leaves and lemon rind and leave to cool and macerate. Pour the cold liquid through a sieve into a bowl, and add lemon juice until you can detect a real tang – freezing will mute the taste if you haven't put in enough lemon. Whisk the egg whites until stiff and incorporate them into the mixture, making sure you have a homogeneous-looking mixture without a layer of liquid under it. Freeze. If you don't have an ice cream maker, beat the mixture after a couple of hours of freezing, paying special attention to the texture. Serve with walnut or almond biscuits.

Walnut Biscuits

Makes about 40

85 ml/3 fl oz walnut oil
125 g/4 oz butter, softened
150 g/5 oz caster sugar
pinch of salt
225 g/8 oz self-raising flour
50–85 g/2–3 oz walnuts, coarsely chopped
1 egg, beaten

Hazelnuts or almonds can be substituted for the walnuts.

Mix all the ingredients together with enough of the egg to bind. Shape the dough into a roll and refrigerate for at least 30 minutes.

Preheat the oven to 190°C/375°F/Gas Mark 5. Slice off very thin circles of dough and bake on a greased baking sheet for 10–15 minutes, until crisp and lightly browned.

Brûléed Blackcurrant Tart

Serves 6

Sweet Pastry (see page 158)
225–275 g/8–10 oz blackcurrants
pinch of ground cinnamon
muscovado sugar, to taste
2 large eggs
2 egg yolks
250 ml/8 fl oz double cream
4 tbsp Kirsch
about 3 tbsp granulated sugar

My favourite cooked blackcurrant recipe is heartier and heavier than those made with raw blackcurrants. This is also delicious made with blueberries.

Preheat the oven to 180°C/350°F/Gas Mark 4. Roll the pastry out thinly and use to line a greased 20 cm/8 inch tart tin with a removable base. Bake blind for 10 minutes, then remove the greaseproof paper and baking beans and return to the oven for a further 10 minutes to dry out.

Meanwhile, put the blackcurrants in a saucepan with 2 tablespoons of water and a pinch of cinnamon, and simmer very briefly. Sweeten to taste with muscovado sugar. In a bowl, beat together the eggs and egg yolks, cream and Kirsch. Add a pinch of muscovado sugar to taste.

Place a single layer of blackcurrants in the pastry case, then pour in the cream mixture and return to the oven for about 30 minutes, until just firm but slightly 'sad' in the centre. Leave to cool.

Just before you want to serve the tart, strew a thin layer of granulated sugar (not too much) over the tart. I have a brilliant blowtorch for bruléeing, which my children gave me one Christmas, but if you don't, protect the pastry edges with a strip of foil, and put the tart under a hot grill until the sugar bubbles and caramelizes. The thin burnt layer marries beautifully with the creamy, fruity middle.

Brûléed blackcurrant tart.

Peach and Almond Crumble Tart

SERVES 6

Shortcrust Pastry (see page 158), baked blind in a 22 cm/9 inch round tin with a removable base
6–7 large peaches, blanched and skinned
3 tbsp unsalted butter
2–3 tbsp caster sugar
a handful of flaked almonds

CRUMBLE TOPPING:
6 tbsp wholemeal flour
6 tbsp ground almonds and a couple of drops of bitter almond essence if you've got it
6 tbsp muscovado sugar
40 g/1½ oz unsalted butter

You can make this crumble tart with any fruit or combination of fruits that appeals. Blackcurrant is delicious, as is blackberry and apple with some ground hazelnuts in the topping mixture, but this is my absolute favourite.

Preheat the oven to 180°C/350°F/Gas Mark 4. Make the crumble topping by mixing the flour, almonds – and almond essence if you are using it – and muscovado sugar and rubbing in the butter; this can be done in a food processor.

Sauté the peaches in the butter with the caster sugar for a few minutes, but don't let them soften too much. Spoon into the tart case, cover with the crumble topping, and bake for 15–20 minutes. Scatter the flaked almonds over the surface and return to the oven for 5–10 minutes to brown – but not burn.

Honey and Lavender Ice Cream

SERVES 6–8

The most unusual and elegant ice cream I have ever made was inspired by the Provençal lavender honey that I used to bring back from the Luberon in the Vaucluse. How to intensify it, as ice creams lose in the freezing if the flavours aren't strong enough? Lavender is the sublime but obvious answer. Delicious served alongside the Peach and Almond Crumble Tart.

Follow the recipe for Vanilla Ice Cream (see page 69), but steep 2 good-sized branches of lavender, 10–13 cm/4–5 inches long, in the single cream you bring to the boil. Continue to simmer, very low, for 20 minutes, then strain the cream on to the yolks and continue to follow the recipe. When the mixture has thickened, pour in about 225 g/8 oz of lavender honey that you have first heated until liquid in a bowl in some simmering water. Stir well into the custard, and freeze in the usual way.

Poached Peaches in an Orange-Flower Sabayon

SERVES 6–8
8–10 peaches
550 ml/18 fl oz water
550 ml/18 fl oz white wine
200 g/7 oz caster sugar
1 orange, sliced
½ a lemon, sliced
1 vanilla pod

FOR THE SABAYON:
6 egg yolks
100 g/3½ oz caster sugar
pinch of salt
125 ml/4 fl oz sweet white wine
4 tbsp fresh lime juice
3 tbsp fresh orange juice
1 tbsp orange-flower water

This was voted the best pudding in The Independent's Cook of the Year competition. French white peaches are the best, but yellow ones are fine. The poaching liquid takes on a wonderful rosy blush from the peach skins.

Put the peaches in a saucepan with the water, wine, sugar, orange, lemon and vanilla pod. Bring to the boil, skim, then simmer very gently for 15–20 minutes. Let the peaches cool in the syrup, then peel off the skins, halve and remove the stones. Reserve the syrup.

For the sabayon, put the egg yolks, caster sugar and salt into a bowl and whisk. Add the wine and 125 ml/4 fl oz of the poaching syrup and whisk in a double boiler over simmering water for about 10 minutes or until the mixture leaves a ribbon trail when the whisk is lifted. Whisk in the lime juice, orange juice and orange-flower water. Spoon the sabayon generously over the peach halves.

As far is food is concerned, my single greatest influence is undoubtedly George Perry-Smith. Jane Grigson and Elizabeth David's books will always be with me, but George I learned from by example. I was too young ever to eat at his famous Hole in the Wall restaurant in Bath, but my two-day honeymoon, picked after scouring the pages of *The Good Food Guide*, was at the place he then took over, Riverside at Helford in Cornwall. It called itself, unpretentiously, a restaurant with rooms, and indeed it was just that. We looked out on to the Helford Estuary from our bedroom above the kitchen, and every morning would smell the inimitable smell of fresh croissants baking. On a good morning, after breakfast on the terrace, strawberries and oranges followed by croissants and homemade apricot jam, one was under obligation to walk the coastal paths to prepare oneself for the evening's feasting.

George's menu changed daily, relying on locally caught fish, wonderful lobsters, crabs, sea bass, turbot and Dover sole, and vegetables from his kitchen garden that rose sheerly behind the house. His fish soup with *aïoli* and *rouille* – 15 years ago nobody else was serving it – his brandade of smoked mackerel, a simple oxtail stewed with grapes, sole Dugléré, his famous Sunday night cold table, his richly delicious walnut treacle tart with a thinner than thin crisp crust – all these dishes tasted of themselves, unfussy yet perfectly cooked and presented. If I were to remember one dish above all others, for its startling yet unobvious originality, it would be his salmon baked in pastry with currants and ginger. On the face of it an extraordinary combination, but a true marriage, with not one ingredient too many. We returned twice a year, in the spring and early autumn, first on our own, then with one child, then with two. They were looked after as well as we were, in a tiny bedroom adjoining ours, where George's wife Heather put a little bed and a cot, and ran the restaurant with consummate charm and ease.

Everyone felt at home, yet everyone felt special, and we all knew that the high point of the day was dinner. All the guests, united in this, could, like at Old Head, have been hand-picked. We all got talking, usually about food, and the following day would more than likely meet on some lost woodland path up a narrow creek reeking of wild garlic and carpeted with bluebells. I cook this dish in the west of Ireland and always think of George and Heather and Riverside, and of the time when they had both retired, and, renting the little cottage they'd kept in Helford, I was finally able to give them dinner. Cooking for the Master is utterly nerve-wracking first time round, but, after that, a pleasure – one hopes on both sides. It goes without saying that the one thing I did not present him with was anything remotely resembling one of his own dishes!

Salmon Baked in Pastry with Currants and Ginger

SERVES 6

1 kg/2½ lb piece of skinned wild salmon, filleted
salt and pepper
3 knobs of ginger in syrup, drained and chopped small
25 g/1 oz currants
125 g/4 oz butter, softened
Shortcrust Pastry (see page 158),made with 450 g/1 lb plain flour
1 egg yolk, beaten, to glaze

SAUCE:
600 ml/1 pint single cream
2 egg yolks
2 tsp French mustard
2 tsp plain flour
125 g/4 oz butter, softened
juice of 1 lemon
½ a small onion, finely chopped
a small bunch of mixed fresh herbs (tarragon, parsley, chervil), chopped

Preheat the oven to 230°C/450°F/Gas Mark 8. Check that no bones remain in the salmon and season on both sides. Incorporate the ginger and currants into the butter, then spread half on the inside of one fillet. Put the other fillet on top and spread the remaining butter over it.

Roll out the pastry and roll and wrap it neatly round the salmon, making sure the edges aren't lumpy. Brush with the egg yolk. Bake in the oven for 30 minutes. If it is a particularly thick piece of salmon, allow another 5 minutes; if tail end, 30 minutes should do it.

To make the sauce, swirl the ingredients together in a blender until green. Heat gently in a double boiler until thickened. Serve in a warm bowl, accompanied by either a cucumber salad or by Jersey new potatoes and Stewed Peas.

Stewed Peas

Put some fresh peas in a saucepan and add chicken stock to come one-third of the way up the peas. Add 1 teaspoon of caster sugar, 1 finely chopped tiny shallot, a large knob of butter and the finely chopped heart of a Cos lettuce. Simmer without a lid until the peas are just tender, by which time the liquid will have reduced somewhat and will coat the peas. Finely chop 3 or 4 small mint leaves, scatter them on top, and serve.

CHAPTER 4

Local Food

Discovering where to shop is always exciting, and invariably the first thing I do when I'm somewhere new. Remembering the paucity of fresh fruit and vegetables that braved the tortuous roads across Ireland in my childhood, I was amazed at the dramatic changes that had occurred over ten years. Westport, the most beautiful small town in Ireland, built entirely to a Georgian design with its two wide main streets, crossed at the top and bottom, where it is also intersected by a beautiful, slow-flowing river, was full of surprises. A fresh fruit and vegetable shop stuffed with exotica, a Thursday morning country market in the town hall, with stacks of freshly baked cakes of soda bread and yeast bread, muffins and crumpets, jams, organic herbs and vegetables, free-range chickens and country butter. And, what has become my favourite delicatessen, Anne and

Preparing smoked salmon at Vincent and Anne Bourke's delicatessen, Westport.

Vincent Bourke's cheese and wine shop. Anne makes the best jams I have ever tasted anywhere, strawberry and redcurrant with whole strawberries; raspberry; blackcurrant or redcurrant jellies and a perfectly textured, bitterish orange marmalade which is wonderful – as well as on toast – with sausages from the award-winning butchers in Newport, also famed for their delicious black and white puddings, or in a Seville Orange and Marmalade Tart (see page 124) that I make in the winter.

Anne sells a terrific selection of Irish cheeses, homemade bread and pâtés, and Vincent smokes the finest sides of wild salmon I have ever tasted. He also smokes his own bacon, so Irish breakfasts before a mountain climb or serious walk take on epic proportions.

Through the mountains and round Killary Bay just an hour and a half southwards is the graceful city of Galway, whose Saturday morning market is always worth the drive. An alley full of stalls glutted with produce of the highest quality; curiously, they are worked by more Germans and Dutch people than Irish – German breads and plaited brioche-style loaves on one stall, home-smoked eels, pickles, and homemade garlicky sausages, some grilling pungently on a brazier, on another, locally made soft Dutch cheeses spiked with garlic or caraway and little goats' cheeses rolled in fresh herbs and garlic, and, most recently, a Provençal stall with olive oil, olives, tapenades, anchovies, honeys, fresh pasta and huge bars of soap.

After a heavy morning's shopping there is only one thing to do, fall into MacDonagh's, a wonderful, old-fashioned fish restaurant, for some Clarenbridge oysters and fish and chips. You can import your glass of Guinness from The Quays bar opposite, and collapse with the cleanest, freshest, salty-juiced oysters, a dozen if you dare.

Opposite is my favourite bookshop Kenny's, run by the Kenny brothers, several rickety floors of new and second-hand books, including an impressively catholic selection of Irish authors, most of whom have passed through the Kenny portals at some stage, and left a signed photograph for the wall. To the back of the shop is a gallery with an eclectic mixture of Irish painters, and if you leave the shop from this side, there is a network of tiny streets full of an amazing range of shops that pour down to the docks, the river and the open sea.

Galway is a city that has a buzz to it, something palpable, tangible, both day and night, with street musicians on every corner, pavement performers, good art, theatre and music, films, fish and food.

Driving back to Mayo through the Twelve Pins, to the next range of darkly beautiful mountains with achingly cold black lakes beneath, I dream up what to cook from the boxes of goods sliding round in the boot, as we dive up and down the twisting road home.

One of my favourites is a dish that is almost the national dish of Ireland, which I first ate in the west with great farming friends, Tommy and Mary Gallagher. When Mary cooks boiled bacon and cabbage, the cabbage is thrown in and cooked with the meat, to absorb all its flavour and juices and exude its own for the accompanying liquor. The best sight, other than the thick hunks of meat that steam pink and succulent with the green cabbage on the plate, is Mary plonking an industrial-sized pot full of floury boiled potatoes on the floor and bending over to attack them with the masher. An old-fashioned pease pudding is a scrumptious accompaniment.

Kenny's bookshop, Galway.

Boiled Bacon with Cabbage

Serves 8

1.8–2.2 kg/4–5 lb unsmoked collar of bacon, without the rind
a selection of chopped vegetables (for example 3 onions, 6 carrots, 2 leeks, 3–4 sticks of celery)
bunch of fresh herbs, tied in a bundle
1.7–2.3 litres/3–4 pints chicken stock or water
1 large green cabbage, chopped and cored

Soak the bacon in cold water for 24 hours, changing the water several times. Put the soaked bacon in a large casserole with the vegetables, herbs and stock or water. Bring just to the boil, skim, turn the heat right down and keep it simmering at a mere bubble, with the lid on, for about 30 minutes.

Add the cabbage and continue to simmer for a further 1 hour (this sounds like a long time, but you are not looking for a crisply *al dente* result, quite the reverse; the slow cooking will soften the cabbage completely). Turn off the heat and allow the meat to 'settle' for 20 minutes, then remove it from the pot, transfer it to a carving board and keep it hot for a further 10 minutes under a tight layer of foil and a cloth.

Using a slotted spoon, lift out the cabbage and discard as much as you can of the other vegetables. Lay a bed of cabbage on each plate, put a couple of thick slices of bacon on top, and serve the cooking liquor in a jug. All you need now is some good mustard and some Champ (see page 40) to soak up the juices.

The same neighbours, Tommy and Mary, usually bring over a whole lamb's liver when they are killing, on the grounds that if I don't cook it, they'd chuck it. Rather than slice it, I put the whole liver in a roasting tin and cook it in the following way. It comes out succulent and juicy, very different from those hideous memories of school dinners: grey, granulated, dried-up meat inside a tough, leathery crust.

Roast Lamb's Liver and Root Vegetables

A WHOLE LAMB'S LIVER IS USUALLY ENOUGH TO SERVE 4

1 whole lamb's liver
a selection of vegetables (for example onions, parsnips, carrots, swede, celeriac)
1 large onion, cut into rings
about 6 tbsp olive oil
salt and pepper
150–300 ml/5–10 fl oz red wine or Dubonnet

Preheat the oven to 180°C/350°F/Gas Mark 4. Trim the liver and peel off the thin outer membrane. Peel the vegetables and chop into good-sized chunks: smallish onions and parsnips can be cut in half, carrots into 5 cm/2 inch lengths, swedes and celeriac into 2.5–5 cm/1–2 inch chunks. Leave the onions raw and parboil the other vegetables for 3–4 minutes, then drain and reserve the water.

Put the large onion rings in a roasting tin, put the liver on top and the prepared vegetables around the liver, and anoint with a generous amount of olive oil. Turn the vegetables to coat them with oil, season, and put the tin in the oven.

After 20 minutes, turn the vegetables and baste the liver. After a further 20 minutes, turn the vegetables again, and pour about 150 ml/5 fl oz of the red wine or Dubonnet over the liver. After a further 10 minutes, baste and check the liver with a skewer; when cooked, it should be pink but not bloody. Depending on its size, it will probably need another 10–20 minutes. Keep basting, and add more wine or Dubonnet if the liquid is evaporating.

When the liver is cooked, transfer the vegetables to a serving dish and keep warm. Wrap the liver in foil and a cloth and place on a carving board. Put the roasting tin over a medium-high heat, bring the wine to the boil, add some of the vegetable cooking water and stir well, scraping all the caramelized oniony bits off the bottom of the tin. Bring back to the boil, then pour the contents of the tin through a sieve into a jug, pressing and rubbing to get as much goodness out of the onions as you can. Carve the liver horizontally into slices and serve with the vegetables and gravy.

I seem to end up cooking a lot of things that are brought – alive or dead – to my doorstep by friends and neighbours.

One of my greatest friends, John Kilcoyne, a mussel fisherman, regularly leaves a sack of fresh Killary mussels, which I use in a seafood risotto, or in a classic chowder that is all the more delicious for the mussels having been hauled up and stripped from their growing ropes the day they are eaten.

Killary Bay mussel chowder.

Killary Bay Mussel Chowder

SERVES 6

150 ml/5 fl oz dry white wine
3 kg/6 lb mussels, cleaned, debarnacled and debearded
large pinch of saffron threads
50 g/2 oz butter
2 potatoes, chopped into 5 mm/¼ inch cubes
2 sticks of celery, finely chopped
2 thin leeks, finely chopped
125 g/4 oz mushrooms, chopped
50 g/2 oz plain flour
900 ml/1½ pints milk
1 bay leaf
salt and pepper
125 g/4 oz smoked streaky bacon, fried in its own fat until crisp, then drained and chopped
a handful of fresh flat-leaf parsley, chopped

The milky, saffrony broth marries beautifully with the soft, salty mussels and contrastingly crisp bacon. This is a meal on its own, perhaps with the addition of some garlic bread dripping with unsalted butter.

Check the mussels as you clean them: if any are open – and do not close when you tap them firmly on the work surface – discard them. Give them a final quick rinse in cold water. Heat the wine in a large saucepan, add the mussels, cover and steam just until the shells open, stirring or shaking the pan frequently. Pour the contents of the pan into a sieve over a bowl, and take the mussels out of their shells, holding them over the sieve to catch the liquid. Discard any mussels that remain closed after cooking. You can refresh the mussels in cold water if you want to keep the flesh tender, but if you cook quickly this won't be necessary. Add the saffron to the hot liquid.

Melt the butter in a saucepan, add the potatoes, celery, leeks and mushrooms and sprinkle with flour, turning to coat the vegetables with flour and butter. Stir in the milk and the strained mussel cooking liquid, add the bay leaf, salt and pepper, and simmer until the vegetables are just tender. Add the mussels and the fried bacon, scatter with the chopped parsley and serve in bowls.

Seafood Risotto

SERVES 6

150–300 ml/5–10 fl oz dry white wine
24 mussels, cleaned, debarnacled and debearded
12 scallops, cleaned
40 g/1½ oz butter
1.5 litres/2½ pints strong fish stock
3 tbsp olive oil
1 large onion, finely chopped
2 sticks of celery, finely chopped
450 g/1 lb arborio rice
a couple of handfuls of fresh peas, if in season
pinch of saffron threads
50 g/2 oz Parmesan cheese, grated
salt and pepper
up to 450 g/1 lb cooked prawns, shelled and deveined
1 tbsp each of chopped fresh chervil and parsley

This is an elegant and beautifully coloured dish, which needs no more by way of accompaniment than the simplest green salad tossed in the very best olive oil. It is the kind of good-tempered dish that responds well to you throwing in whatever seafood you can lay your hands on. The real prerequisite is some good strong fish stock, which I usually make with an assortment of crab, lobster and prawn and shrimp shells. Reducing it to strengthen the flavour once you've discarded the shells, bones and vegetables is a good idea.

Heat a little of the wine in a saucepan, add the mussels, cover and steam just until the shells open. Remove the mussels and put to one side. Cook the scallops by slicing the white flesh into two or three discs, leaving the corals whole, and sautéing the white parts in a little of the butter for 30 seconds on each side, the coral for 30 seconds altogether. Bring the fish stock to the boil and keep it at simmering point to add to the rice.

Heat the oil in a large, heavy pan, add the onion and celery and cook over a low heat until they have softened and turned golden. Stir in the rice and keep stirring to coat, until it begins to look translucent. Turn up the heat and add about 150 ml/5 fl oz of the wine. When it has been absorbed, start adding the hot stock, a ladle or two at a time. Stir the liquid in carefully, and let it simmer until it has been almost absorbed before you add more, and the peas if you are using them. Keep adding the stock a little at a time, and with the last ladleful add the saffron.

After about 20–25 minutes the rice will be slightly resistant to the bite, but almost tender. Stir in a small lump of butter, the grated Parmesan, salt and pepper. Add the prawns, mussels and scallops. Scatter the herbs over the top, and if the dish doesn't appear beautifully liquid, add a final ladleful of fish stock. Season to taste and serve in bowls.

Leek, Potato and Oatmeal Tart

SERVES 6

125 g/4 oz wholemeal or plain white flour
125 g/4 oz rolled oats
pinch of salt
125 g/4 oz butter, chilled and cut into small pieces

FILLING:
25 g/1 oz butter
the white part of 4 thick leeks, sliced 3 mm/⅛ inch thick
1 clove garlic, finely chopped
salt and pepper
1 large egg and 1 egg yolk
150 ml/5 fl oz single cream
pinch of grated nutmeg
3–4 potatoes, boiled until just tender, then sliced
1 tbsp chopped fresh thyme
50 g/2 oz strong Cheddar cheese and 50 g/2 oz Parmesan cheese, grated and mixed

Leeks and oatmeal are as much a part of Ireland's culinary heritage as potatoes. My idea was to combine all three in one dish, and this is the result.

Preheat the oven to 190°C/375°F/Gas Mark 5. To make the pastry, put the flour, oats and salt in a bowl, add the butter and rub it in lightly. Add just enough cold water to bind the mixture together. Roll out and use to line a 22 or 30 cm/9 or 12 inch tart tin. Bake the pastry blind for 10 minutes. Remove the greaseproof paper and beans.

Meanwhile, for the filling, heat the butter in a frying pan and sauté the leeks and garlic until softened, then season them. Whisk together the egg, yolk and cream and season with salt, pepper and nutmeg. Spread the leeks over the pastry base, add a layer of potatoes, the thyme, more seasoning, and half the cheese, then add a second layer of potatoes. Pour over the cream and egg mixture, season, scatter on the rest of the cheese, and return to the oven for about 25 minutes until the top is deliciously browned. Serve this with a Provençale Tomato Salad, a wonderfully gutsy and fresh acompaniment.

Provençale Tomato Salad

SERVES 4–6

The dressing should not be made more than half an hour before you are going to serve it, or it will turn purple.

Blanch and skin 450 g/1 lb tomatoes, slice them and arrange in rows on a flat dish. Leave in the fridge until you are nearly ready to serve the salad. Into a food processor or liquidizer put 150 ml/5 fl oz of mixed olive oil and walnut oil, 1 tablespoon of walnuts, 1 clove of garlic and 1 heaped tablespoon each of chopped fresh flat-leaf parsley and fresh basil. Add salt and pepper. Blend briefly to amalgamate, pour over the chilled tomatoes and serve.

You would think it would be easy to lay your hands on organic or at least free-range hens in Mayo – not so. Neighbours rear their own ducks and hens, and geese and turkeys for Christmas, but if you want to buy them, other than the Christmas birds, it's not that easy. Local supermarkets sell only the pallid, intensively reared chickens, with flesh that feels and tastes like it's been knitted. The Westport country market has a few hens that you can order, and one old-fashioned butcher I know 1½ hours away in Galway has them, where I stock up if I'm staying long.

The next recipe is so easy a child could cook it, and is one of those dishes that is aeons more delicious than the sum of its parts would suggest. Curiously, although the garlic is cooked in vegetable quantity, all the strength is dissipated in the cooking, so, far from lingering on the breath or causing indigestion, it takes on a strangely subtle and delicate flavour, enhanced by the bird's own juices.

Maureen Bourke at the children's races on the beach during our local community festival. Summer '95.

Chicken Smothered in Garlic

SERVES 6

1 large chicken, 1.8–2.2 kg/
4–5 lb, with its liver and giblets
1 lemon, halved
3 tbsp olive oil
40–50 cloves garlic, peeled
salt and pepper
2–3 sprigs of thyme

Preheat the oven to 150°C/300°F/Gas Mark 2. Remove and reserve the liver and giblets and tuck the lemon halves inside the chicken. Heat the oil in a casserole and gently brown the chicken on all sides. Add the garlic and turn the cloves to coat them with oil. Turn the bird breast down, season, add the giblets (not the liver) and thyme and put on the lid. Cook in the oven for 1½ hours, then turn the bird breast up, put the lid back on and cook for another 30 minutes.

Lift the chicken out of the casserole, holding it on end so all the delicious juices run into the pot, then put it on a carving board and wrap in foil. Discard the giblets and add the liver to the casserole to cook briefly, either cut in thin strips, or mash it as you go. Add the juices from the resting bird to the pot, carve, and serve with some of the cloves of garlic on each plate, along with a moat of golden juice. Mashed potato or rice should be served with it, and a couple of contrastingly coloured vegetables, say carrots and spinach or courgettes.

Sautéd Courgettes

Coarsely grate some courgettes and cook them in a little olive oil over a low heat until just tender. Squeeze ½ a lemon over them, and season with salt and pepper.

Carrots Vichy

Slice some carrots into fingers and put in a saucepan. Pour in some chicken stock or water to come halfway up the carrots, add 1 teaspoon of molasses sugar and a lump of butter, and boil hard until all that is left of the liquid is a thick, buttery coating. Shake the carrots to distribute the coating evenly and, if you like, add some chopped fresh chives or thyme.

Poulet Vallée d'Auge

Serves 4

125 g/4 oz butter
675 g/1½ lb apples, peeled, cored and sliced
2–3 tsp light muscovado sugar
1.5–2 kg/3–4½ lb chicken
3–4 tbsp Calvados
300 ml/10 fl oz chicken stock
200 ml/7 fl oz double cream
salt and pepper
½ a lemon

When you feel like an unctuously rich dish, pheasant, guinea fowl or chicken cooked à la Normande is the perfect answer. This recipe, named after a river valley in Normandy, combines the three ingredients that typify the region: cream, Calvados and apples. You can use good rough cider instead if you don't have any Calvados.

Preheat the oven to 180°C/350°F/Gas Mark 4. Heat about half the butter in a frying pan and fry 450 g/1 lb of the apple slices. As they begin to soften, scatter 1–2 teaspoons of the sugar over them, turning to coat them in the juices. Arrange them in the bottom of a casserole. Add the chicken to the frying pan and brown on all sides, then add the Calvados and set light to it with a taper. When the flames die down, put the chicken, breast down, into the casserole. Add the stock to the frying pan and stir to deglaze it, then pour it over the bird with half the cream. Put the lid on the casserole and cook in the oven for about 1 ¼–1 ½ hours, turning the bird over halfway through the cooking time.

Take the bird out of the casserole, transfer to a carving board and wrap in foil. Fry the remaining apple slices in the remaining butter, sprinkling with sugar, until they are caramelized but still just firm. Add the juices from the resting chicken to the casserole, together with the remaining cream, bring to the boil, then rub through a sieve. Season the sauce and add a good squeeze of lemon juice, and serve separately. The chicken should be carved and laid on a bed of rice with the caramelized apples alongside it.

Crisp, lightly boiled green beans with a few toasted pine nuts scattered over them is the only accompaniment you will need, and adds colour to the ivory tones of the other ingredients.

I first encountered an *aïoli* at a restaurant in the village of Murs, perched high above Gordes in Provence. Our two eldest children, tiny at the time, played in the street, while we assaulted an Everest of salted cod, surrounded by the clear, earthy flavours of the vegetables that had all been cooked separately and sat steaming alongside the fish: artichokes, green beans, fennel, carrots and potatoes in their skins. A large bowl of pungently sticky ointment rested on the side, a Provençal *aïoli*, heaving with new season's garlic. It was a dish I returned to, at the same restaurant, for several years, as I did with their *bourride*, a fish stew into which the *aïoli* is stirred at the last moment. I make it with chicken, a great vehicle for the strong flavours that permeate it: garlic, saffron and tomato. It is easy to prepare both the stew and the *aïoli* hours in advance, effecting the final marriage of the two minutes just before you want to eat, so it's great for holidays and entertaining.

Bourride of Chicken

Serves 4

3 tbsp olive oil
the white part of 2 thick leeks, chopped
225 g/8 oz carrots, chopped
225 g/8 oz onions, chopped
2–3 cloves garlic, chopped
1 small chicken, 1.5–1.6 kg /3–3½ lb, skinned and cut into 4 joints
4 plum tomatoes, skinned, seeded and chopped
2 sprigs of thyme
2 bay leaves
large pinch of saffron threads
strips of peel from 1 orange
150 ml/5 fl oz dry white wine
salt and pepper
1 tbsp each of chopped fresh parsley and chives

Preheat the oven to 150°C/300°F/Gas Mark 2. Heat the oil in a casserole and sauté the leeks, carrots, onions and garlic until softened. Add the chicken joints, tomatoes, herbs, a good pinch of saffron and the orange peel. Simmer together for 10 minutes, then add the wine and seasoning. Cover and cook in the oven for 30 minutes.

Meanwhile, make the *aïoli* (see next page). When the chicken is cooked, remove it from the casserole and keep it warm. Stir the *aïoli* into the casserole and bring it just to the point of boiling, then immediately remove it from the heat. Pour it over the chicken, scatter with parsley and chives and serve with rice.

Aïoli

4 cloves garlic
salt and pepper
3 egg yolks
juice of ½ a lemon
450 ml/15 fl oz olive oil

Crush the garlic and a little salt firmly with a pestle in a large bowl until it is creamy. Beat in the egg yolks, then the lemon juice. Whisk in the oil, a drop at a time at first, then in a thin, steady stream as you would for mayonnaise. Season, taste, and add a little more lemon juice if you like.

Aïoli is wonderful with fish, too, particularly firm, white-fleshed fish such as cod, hake or monkfish, that benefit from a full-bodied, strong-flavoured sauce. If you are making a fish stew with an assortment of fish cooked briefly in chunks in a good fish stock, stir in the *aïoli* at the end of the cooking time, as for the *bourride*, and serve it with an accompanying *rouille*.

Rouille

1 small can (200 g/7 oz) pimientos, drained
1 clove garlic
2 fresh red chilli peppers, chopped and seeded, or ½–1 tsp harissa, depending on how hot you like your rouille
2 tbsp olive oil
salt

Swirl everything together in a liquidizer or food processor, and serve in a bowl alongside a fish stew or soup, so people can spoon it on top of their *aïoli*.

Some like the addition of some crisply fried garlic croûtons, although I find the oil content too much. If you don't, fry some 2.5 cm/1 inch squares of day-old bread in olive oil until really golden, drain them on kitchen paper, then rub them with a cut clove of garlic. They can be scattered over the stew or soup with some grated Parmesan cheese.

It is even more difficult to procure good fish than good meat in the west of Ireland, unless you are prepared to catch them yourself. My near neighbour, Michael Viney, who writes a column for the *Irish Times* about life and wildlife in the west, used to put lines down on the beach at low tide, and return after the tide to see what flat fish had bitten. Otherwise you need a boat.

When a great friend, Tor Belfrage, came out to escape

OVERLEAF: *John Kilcoyne on his boat.*

London and what would have been the second anniversary of her marriage to Julian, had he not died, we decided that the day itself should be a celebration, and that we should do something that would have made Jules hysterical with laughter. We decided to go shark fishing. John Kilcoyne, whose own boat was busy, and who, with his wife Merci, was decidedly keen on a busman's holiday for which he didn't have to take responsibility, tried to find us one. The island that I look out on to, Inish Turk, has several good boats, and we first rang Mick O'Toole, a fisherman on the island, but they were all busy. John K checked up all round Old Head and Achill, but there was a shark-fishing competition going on, and there wasn't a boat to be had. What's more, the unnaturally halcyon summer appeared to be changing; the weather forecast was for rain and a Force 4–5 gale. Undeterred, John finally tracked down a little boat at Cleggan in Connemara; its willing owner, who had all the right equipment, had caught a shark two weeks previously.

We set off from Cleggan harbour for the open sea, feeling a bit like extras for *Jaws*, but even before we reached it the waves were slapping at the little boat with a firm hand, and some of us felt decidedly uneasy. John K, like a true professional, was bracing himself for what lay ahead with nose-to-toe yellow oilskins. Tor and I looked at each other – we were in jeans and gym shoes – and the first big wave that swept the deck clean saw our toes turning purple after a total immersion baptism. The open sea was worse. The waves were over ten feet tall, and we had to plough through them, taking them roller-coaster style with barely a breath to recover in before the next. The strange thing about fear is that when you are at the heart of it, it strikes you as totally pointless. Merci, Tor and I clung together, begging John K to get the boat turned round and headed for home. We had brought our eldest two children: Miranda was clearly enjoying every minute of it, Harry was hunkered down beside me, head low, speechless, grim-faced, trying not to think about what he'd had for breakfast.

The other strange thing about fear is that if it goes on relentlessly for long enough you can't go on taking it so seriously and, perversely, you start enjoying it. An hour later, perching precariously at angles of 60 degrees with our feet planted apart, martial arts style, for balance, we had the mackerel lines out. The engine was switched off and we rested parallel to the mainland and the island of Inis Boffin, alternately in the troughs then breasting the peaks of the waves, pulling up four or five fish at a time: mackerel, cod and pollack.

At lunch time we landed on Inis Boffin, drank a skinful of Stagg – a fruity Irish cider – and Guinness, and Merci and I danced a couple of Irish dances to try and assuage the penetrating chill. The weather had not improved, and our skipper deemed it unsafe to head for the sharky waters beyond the islands in the open Atlantic, so we headed hard by the now unpopulated island of Inis Shark, and carried on fishing. This time we landed an extraordinary mixture, including a thornback ray, its leopard-skin back peppered with sharp, thorny excrescences like the most savage of rose bushes. Introducing it to the deck, Harry, fascinated by its great googly eyes and opening and closing mouth, proceeded to throw it salt and vinegar crisps 'so that it would taste better'. Then up came a baby octopus who proceeded to march across the deck, its small orb of a head changing colour, glowing pink then green like a mini traffic light.

When we arrived home that night, even after an hour on dry land we still rolled around as if we were on deck. I set to work with the thornback ray, hacking off its wings and preparing it for the pot, for Skate with an Anchovy and Caper Sauce.

Skate with an Anchovy and Caper Sauce

SERVES 4

allow a generous 225 g/8 oz or more wing of skate per person
3–4 tbsp white wine vinegar
a bunch of fresh thyme
2 bay leaves
large pinch of sea salt

ANCHOVY AND CAPER SAUCE:
1 small can (50 g/2 oz) anchovies in olive oil, drained
50 g/2 oz butter
about 2 tsp olive oil
1 small onion or 2 shallots, finely chopped
150 ml/5 fl oz dry white wine
2–3 tbsp double cream
2 tbsp mixed chopped fresh herbs (dill, flat-leaf parsley, chervil)
2 tbsp capers, thoroughly rinsed
pepper
½ a lemon

This is one of those magical recipes, not time-consuming, not unduly difficult, which seems to impress well beyond the level of its complexity – a dish to grace either a serious dinner party or an everyday supper. When you buy skate, smell it: the first hint of ammonia means it's on the turn. It should be firm-textured. It benefits hugely from a piquant, slightly salty accompaniment.

Put the vinegar, thyme, bay leaves and sea salt in a wide, shallow pan, add about 8 cm/3 inches of water and bring to the boil. Add the skate, bring the liquid back to a faint bubble and simmer for 10 minutes.

Meanwhile, make the sauce. Swirl the anchovies and butter to a paste in a food processor. Heat the oil in a small saucepan and sauté the onion or shallots until softened, then add the wine and boil to reduce considerably. Add a couple of tablespoons of the skate's poaching liquid and reduce again. Whisk in little knobs of the anchovy butter until the sauce has emulsified, then add the cream, and stir it well in to amalgamate. Add the chopped herbs, the capers, some pepper – but no salt, as the anchovies will provide it – and squeeze on lemon juice to taste.

Take off the ray's leopard-skin jacket – or the skate's ermine one! Once it is on the plate, liberally anoint the fish with the sauce and serve with something like mildly bitter Braised Endives and mashed potato.

Braised Endives

Lay 1–2 heads of chicory (Belgian endive) per person in an earthenware or similar baking dish. Dribble over some olive oil, salt and pepper. Cover and cook in a moderate oven, 160°C/325°F/Gas Mark 3, for 1 hour. Squeeze the juice of a lemon over the chicory, return to the oven for 30 minutes, then serve straight from the baking dish with their juices.

Caponata

SERVES 4

4 aubergines
salt and pepper
4–6 tbsp olive oil
1 onion, sliced
1 clove garlic, chopped
6 plum tomatoes, skinned, seeded and chopped
2 tbsp capers, rinsed
50 g/2 oz pitted green olives
3 sticks of celery, chopped
4 tbsp wine vinegar
1 tbsp molasses sugar
3 tbsp chopped fresh parsley

Capers are a classic with skate, and a warm Caponata – a sort of sweet and sour aubergine salad with capers – is another delicious accompaniment for plain, poached skate wings.

Cut the aubergines into cubes, sprinkle them with salt and leave for 30 minutes. Rinse thoroughly and pat them dry. Fry the aubergine cubes in olive oil until tender and brown, then drain them thoroughly on kitchen paper. Add a little more oil to the pan if necessary and gently sauté the onion and garlic until golden. Add the tomatoes and simmer for 15–20 minutes. Blanch the capers, olives and celery briefly in boiling water, drain, then add them to the tomato sauce together with the vinegar, sugar, salt and pepper.

Simmer for another 20 minutes, stirring from time to time, then pour over the aubergines and mix well. Leave until just warm, and add the parsley just before serving.

CHAPTER 5

Entertaining

A close neighbour, Rosemary Garvey, entertains with the consummate ease that I suppose one should expect of someone who has had to, for professional reasons, for a large part of her life. Her husband, Terence Garvey, was an ambassador, and Rosemary, now in her seventies, has lived all over the world and assimilated, not unnaturally, a myriad of cultures.

She is able to put together a room full of people, from the very young to the very old, of disparate interests, political positions, beliefs and persuasions, and make it work. And make it appear that the whole party was no effort, which is a fundamental skill in relaxing your guests. People come, people go. The large kitchen with its turf fire houses the food and some of the guests, the sitting room the rest. People move between the two, children go outside, come back in, dogs and a cat appear, and there will be

Seamus Heneghan, accordian player and fisherman, with friends in a local bar.

OVERLEAF AND BELOW: *Tug of war at our community festival.*

anything up to two dozen people, from diplomats and politicians, to writers, artists and academics, family, neighbours, and whatever waifs and strays are staying with them.

I first met Rosemary as a child, and didn't see her again until I bought my house nearby. In her quiet way she has made many things happen for us, her neighbours and her friends, and all with the minimum of fuss or desire for the gesture to be recognized. When we met again after two decades, an apocryphal story came to mind that my father had told us, and that had assumed the status of legend in our household. To begin with, I wasn't sure whether to remind Rosemary of it, or whether she would even remember it, but it did occur to me that if she did, her version could well be different.

My father rarely lost his temper. When he did, all in the vicinity knew about it, the lowest profile wouldn't be low enough, and the brief storm could mean the dining-room table being split. But then, like a tornado, it was over as soon as it had arrived, no grudge or grievance born or sustained.

My parents set out with Rosemary and Terence and assorted friends and children for a walk that would take them across beaches and headland and bog and stream. Papa led, with his prized new camera round his neck. The party arrived at a stream that might have been jumpable in their youth, but, as is so often the case, was tantalizingly just beyond their stretch. My father's Aunt 'Knos', who virtually reared him after his mother died, was forever saying 'Don't be bold, Master Cecil.' She shouldn't have bothered: he had a streak of bloody-minded daring, in itself a challenge to others, that meant he would always take a risk if it looked like coming off. As I was told the story, the Garvey clan insisted that the stream was passable. He rolled his trousers up and took a step, and was only up to his knees. The next step took him in up to his waist. The bank was a couple of steps away. He took another step and went in over his head.

The camera was ruined, as was the day, and when I was a child the incident and the Garveys were often referred to in tandem. Of course, Rosemary remembered the event, and with glee. The two of us have since looked through the photograph albums in the hope of finding some record of the day – before the disaster.

Since spending so much time in Mayo I have met a huge selection of the friends and relations who seem to flow constantly in and out of Rosemary's house and, consequently, have entertained a good number of them myself. Rosemary's practised informality may well be a talent rather than a skill you can acquire, but a cold buffet, provided there is a chair for everyone – or the floor for children – is definitely the answer. If buffets conjure up soggy quiche, rice salad, catering packs of coleslaw and potato salad, and paper-thin slices of a pallid, factory-farmed beast, think again. The buffet is one occasion when, curiously, many different tastes, textures, combinations and colours can, if well thought out, come together and make a perfect whole. Everything is built around one central dish, which in summer is usually a wild salmon, poached or baked *en papillote*, and in winter a huge baked ham with homemade Cumberland Sauce (see page 109). Here are some of the dishes I surround them with. The Spiced Lentil Salad I make as a variation of Dal (see page 146) and the Provençale Tomato Salad (see page 87) are both dishes you can add to the feast.

Beetroot, Broad Bean, Artichoke & Smoked Bacon Salad with an Anchovy Dressing

SERVES 4 AS A STARTER OR LUNCH DISH; ADJUST THE QUANTITIES FOR A BUFFET

6 small raw beetroot
1 lemon, halved
4 globe artichokes
450 g/1 lb shelled broad beans – the baby ones
4 duck or hen eggs
125 g/4 oz oak-smoked bacon rashers, cut into small strips
2–3 tbsp chopped fresh parsley

ANCHOVY DRESSING:
4–5 tbsp olive oil
450 g/1 lb mild onions, thinly sliced
3 cloves garlic, thinly sliced
1 small can (50 g/2 oz) anchovies in olive oil, or the salted kind, soaked in cold water
1 tbsp white wine vinegar
pepper

This is a beautifully earthy dish with a wonderful combination of flavours and colours. In winter, use chopped potato instead of the broad beans; don't worry if you can't get artichokes, the salad is just as good without them. Keep all the vegetables separate on the plate.

Preheat the oven to 150°C/300°F/Gas Mark 2. Scrub the beetroot but do not peel them. Place on a baking sheet in the oven for about 2 hours or until tender. Peel off the skins, and cut the beetroot into cubes or thin wedges.

Bring a large saucepan of water to the boil, squeeze in the lemon juice and drop in the lemon halves. Add the artichokes and boil until the leaves come away easily. Leave to cool, strip off the leaves, scrape out the 'choke' and trim off the stem, leaving the heart, which is all you use in this recipe. Cook the broad beans in boiling salted water until *al dente*, then skin any that look large and toughish.

Boil the eggs for 6–8 minutes, so that the yolks remain soft; you might like to boil an extra egg first, to test the cooking time. Sauté the bacon until really frizzled; you don't need any fat to do this.

Meanwhile, make the dressing. Heat the oil in a heavy-bottomed frying pan, add the onions and garlic, cover the pan and sweat until thoroughly softened, golden and wilted, which will take about 20 minutes. Add the drained anchovies and put the whole lot into a liquidizer or food processor with the vinegar. Blend until smooth and season with pepper.

Shell the eggs and cut them in half. Arrange the vegetables in sections on a pretty plate, sprinkle the bacon on top of the broad beans and arrange the halved eggs around the edge of the plate. Pour on the warm dressing and scatter with a generous amount of chopped parsley.

Salade Cauchoise

Again, adjust the quantities to your party; this amount is for one person. You don't need to be too precise about quantities – or even ingredients: if you don't have spring onions, use chives, shallots or onions.

Finely shred about 50 g/2 oz cooked ham into long thin strips, and put in a bowl with a stick of finely chopped celery. Add 1 tablespoon of chopped spring onions, and another of well broken walnuts, then season with salt, pepper and a clove of crushed garlic. Add a few boiled tiny new potatoes if you want to make the dish more substantial. Mix well, and bind with some homemade mayonnaise that you have thinned with cream or milk.

Rillettes de Tours

SERVES 4–6 AS A STARTER OR LUNCH DISH; 8–10 AS PART OF A BUFFET

900 g/2 lb belly pork
1 wineglass of dry white wine
4–6 cloves garlic, crushed
pinch of grated nutmeg
salt and pepper
450 g/1 lb pork fat

You need only a small quantity of this rich, coarsely textured potted meat, which keeps beautifully in the fridge. The most common fault is to either underseason or undercook the meat.

Take the rind off the belly pork and put to one side. Remove and discard the bones, and cut the meat into 2.5 cm/1 inch chunks. Put them into a Pyrex or any non-aluminium dish. Pour the wine over them, then add the garlic, nutmeg and seasoning. Cover and bake slowly in a very low oven, 110°C/225°F/Gas Mark ¼, for at least 5 hours or until the meat is virtually falling to pieces.

Sprinkle the rind with salt and roast it in a hot oven, 200°C/400°F/Gas Mark 6, until crisp. Leave to cool on a rack set over a plate to catch any residue that runs off it. Chop the rind finely. Melt the pork fat and strain it. Shred the meat roughly, using two forks, and mix it with its juices and garlic; mix in the chopped roasted rind and its juices. Put into small pots or jars, or one larger earthenware dish. When cool, pour the pork fat over it to seal the top. Serve with hunks of crusty bread, and some olives, gherkins and lettuce.

Green Beans in an Egg and Lemon Sauce

Use the long, thin, Kenyan beans which need topping but not tailing; 450 g/1 lb of beans will serve 4–6.

Cook the beans until just tender in boiling salted water. Drain them, keeping a ladleful of the cooking water, to which you whisk in the juice of 1 lemon and 2 egg yolks. Heat cautiously, whisking all the time, until the sauce thickens miraculously and froths up. Pour warm over the beans, and you have a Greek-style avgolemeno dish. Grind some pepper over the dish, and leave to cool.

Fasoulia

SERVES 6 AS A LUNCH OR SUPPER DISH;
10–12 AS PART OF A BUFFET

450 g/1 lb dried butter beans
2 large onions
4–6 tbsp olive oil
3 cloves garlic, chopped
3–4 tomatoes, skinned, seeded and chopped
2 tbsp tomato purée
½ a lemon
3–4 tbsp chopped fresh parsley

The Greeks are particularly good at warm bean dishes, semi-stew, semi-salad in concept. For a winter buffet there is nothing nicer to accompany your gammon than a slightly oily, tomatoey butter bean dish.

Soak the beans in cold water overnight. Drain, rinse and put them in a large saucepan with fresh water to cover the beans. Bring to the boil and simmer for about 2 hours, or until tender. Drain, reserving some of the cooking liquid.

Slice the onions into thin rings and stew gently in about half the olive oil with the garlic. Add the tomatoes, tomato purée and the beans, with just enough of the cooking liquid to thin the sauce without making it liquid. Leave to cool slightly, then pour some olive oil and a generous squeeze of lemon juice over the beans and turn them gently. Serve warm, scattered with chopped parsley.

Baked Stuffed Field Mushrooms

Serves 4–6 as a starter or lunch dish; 8–10 as part of a buffet

450 g/1 lb large, flat mushrooms
4–6 tbsp olive oil
1 fennel bulb, finely chopped
1 stick of celery, finely chopped
1 small onion, finely chopped
2 cloves garlic, finely chopped
1 tbsp chopped fresh thyme
a handful of coarsely grated Parmesan cheese
a handful of chopped fresh parsley
a handful of fresh brown breadcrumbs
salt and pepper
about 150 ml/5 fl oz red wine
about 150 ml/5 fl oz chicken stock or water

Very good for the vegetarians in your party, this is a perfect buffet dish, because the stuffing can be cooked in advance, the dish then assembled ready for the oven, and it is something you can happily serve warm rather than hot.

Preheat the oven to 180°C/350°F/Gas Mark 4. Wipe the mushrooms clean of earth with a damp cloth. Break off the stalks and chop the stalks finely. Make a duxelles by heating half the oil in a frying pan and sautéing the fennel, celery, onion and mushroom stalks with the garlic and thyme.

Mix together the Parmesan, parsley and breadcrumbs for the topping.

Put a tablespoon of stuffing into each mushroom and season, then cover with a layer of the topping. Place in a roasting tin and dribble the remaining oil over the top. Put a couple of ladles of red wine and the same of water or stock into the roasting tin, and cook in the oven until the mushrooms can be pierced easily with a knife, and their tops are golden and crusty. Check after 20–30 minutes that the wine and water hasn't been absorbed – if it has, ladle in some more.

Watercress and Blue Cheese Salad with a Toasted Sesame Dressing

Toasted sesame seeds transform the most mundane of salads, are brilliant scattered over a spinach, frizzled bacon and avocado salad, and equally good with the salty, peppery flavours of watercress, rocket and blue cheese. In Ireland I use Cashel Blue, but you can use anything from Roquefort to Lanark Blue.

Wash and drain the watercress and rocket and place in a serving dish. Toast a good handful of sesame seeds in the oven until they are brown but not burnt, which happens very quickly. Add some crumbled blue cheese to the salad. Make a simple dressing with good olive oil and balsamic vinegar, and toss the salad. Scatter the sesame seeds on top.

Spiced Rice Salad

SERVES 4–6 AS A STARTER OR LUNCH DISH;
8–10 AS PART OF A BUFFET

a handful of wild rice
450 g/1 lb brown basmati rice
a cinnamon stick
1 tsp turmeric
fresh ginger, about 5 cm/2 in long
1 tsp ground cloves
1 tsp grated nutmeg
6–7 coriander seeds, crushed
a bunch of spring onions, finely chopped
125 g/4 oz fresh peas, if in season, cooked until tender
2–3 tbsp olive oil
salt and pepper
½ a lemon
2–3 tbsp pine nuts
a handful of raisins

OPTIONAL:
finely chopped coriander

Bring a large saucepan of boiling water to the boil and throw in the wild rice. After 10 minutes, add the basmati rice, cinnamon stick, turmeric and ginger and boil for about 40 minutes. Drain the rice and remove the ginger and cinnamon.

Immediately stir in the cloves, nutmeg and coriander seeds, then the spring onions and cooked peas if you're using them. Moisten the rice with olive oil, but not too liberally, and season with black pepper, salt and a squeeze of lemon juice.

Roast the pine nuts in the oven for about 10 minutes or until pale brown. Meanwhile, soak the raisins in boiling water for 10 minutes until they swell. Drain and scatter over the rice, with the pine nuts. You can add some finely chopped coriander if you like.

Ceviche of Salmon

SERVES 6–8

675 g/1½ lb skinned and filleted piece from the centre of the salmon
175 ml/6 fl oz dry white wine
juice of 1 lime
juice of ½ an orange
juice of ½ a lemon
1 small onion, sliced in thin rings
1 small clove garlic, sliced
salt and pepper
4 tbsp olive oil

Using a very sharp knife, slice the salmon, straight from the fridge, into 5 mm/ ¼ inch slices, and put into a container with a lid – an old plastic ice cream container is ideal. Add all the other ingredients, cover and refrigerate. Turn the salmon occasionally, or shake the container gently. The dish is ready to eat after about 8 hours, and it will keep well for about 2 days if you remember to remove the onion and garlic after the first day so that they don't overwhelm it.

To serve, strain off the marinade and put a tablespoon of the Cucumber and Avocado Sambal (see page 67) alongside the fish, and some Brown Soda Bread (see page 26) if you like.

Potato Mayonnaise

It must be my Irish blood, but to my mind all the best buffets include a good potato salad.

Use the best potatoes you can find – Pink Fir Apples, Jersey Royals, Ratte or Charlotte are the best – and boil them in their skins. Dress them while still very warm with a good mayonnaise made with 2 egg yolks, a large teaspoon of grainy mustard, and a couple of tablespoons of best olive oil; the rest of the oil – about 125 ml/4 fl oz – should be cold-pressed safflower or sunflower oil. Squeeze in some lemon juice, and thin with milk or the juices from a salmon if you have just cooked it *en papillote*. Season to taste, add a handful of finely chopped spring onions, and pour over the potatoes, turning them gently to coat them. A good scattering of chives or parsley adds colour, or if you feel like something more unusual, some finely chopped lovage gives a slightly musty, curry-like flavour.

Cumberland Sauce

1 orange
1 lemon
225 g/8 oz redcurrant jelly
1 tsp French mustard
50 ml/2 fl oz port
salt and pepper

OPTIONAL:
Ground cloves, nutmeg or ginger

If you are serving a dish of thickly cut ham from a whole one you have cooked, the syrupy, fruity accompaniment of a good Cumberland sauce is perfect. Swaddles Green Farm, at Buckland St Mary in Somerset, sells either green ham, or their own cured and smoked ones, steeped in a wonderful brine which they have managed to perfect without the addition of saltpetre. You can order them by telephone or fax and have them delivered; they are the best and most succulent I have ever tasted.

First comes the time-consuming part. Peel the orange and lemon with a potato peeler so you have virtually no bitter pith. Shred the peel as finely as you can, and blanch in boiling water for a few minutes. Drain and set aside.

In a saucepan, heat the jelly and mustard together until well melted, add the port, and whisk until hot. Add the orange and lemon juice, season to taste, and if you feel like a bit of spice add a pinch of ground cloves, nutmeg or ginger. Stir in the peel and simmer for 5 minutes. Pour into a bowl or jar and keep in the fridge until you want to use it; it will keep for several weeks.

OVERLEAF: *Ingredients for ceviche of salmon.*

CONTRÔLÉE
NOBLE

Puddings for buffets should be kept as simple as possible, and confined to those you can prepare in advance. In summer a compote of mixed berries and currants served with a homemade ice cream, in winter a warm Hazelnut and Apricot Tart (see opposite) or, after Christmas, mince pies made with homemade mincemeat, unsueted, full of vine fruits, chopped almonds, grated apple and carrot, brandy and raw brown sugar, with some orange rind stirred in, and some orange juice and ground almonds in the pastry. Traditional food, tasting not quite how you are used to it.

Lemon Tart

SERVES 10–12

Sweet Pastry (see page 158), made with 325 g/12 oz butter, 100 g/3½ oz caster sugar and 2 egg yolks
6 lemons
9 egg yolks
325 g/12 oz vanilla caster sugar
300 ml/10 fl oz double cream
about 3 tbsp caster sugar for the top

This is perfect in summer or winter. Everyone has a recipe for it, and I must have tried 20 different versions of varying degrees of sweetness, setness, consistency, with and without adding ground almonds, rhubarb and caramelized slices of lemon. I think this is the best of the lot, meltingly light and lemony, with the top barely set and lemon-curd-like. Since my children gave me a lethal-looking blowtorch for Christmas, I can even scorch the top evenly with sugar and make the finished dish look almost professional.

Preheat the oven to 200°C/400°F/Gas Mark 6. Roll out the pastry and use to line a 30 cm/12 inch round tart tin with a removable base. Bake the pastry case blind for 10 minutes, remove the greaseproof paper and beans and cook for a further 10 minutes.

Meanwhile, finely grate the rind of 2 lemons, and squeeze the juice of all 6, and set aside. Whisk together the egg yolks and the sugar until thoroughly mixed. Add the lemon juice and rind and continue whisking, then whisk in the cream. Taste, and if it is not quite sweet enough add a further 25–50 g/1–2 oz of sugar. Transfer the mixture to a jug.

As soon as the pastry case is cooked, very carefully pour the filling in while the tart case remains where it is on the central shelf of the oven. The pastry case will be sufficiently sealed in the heat to prevent the filling from seeping through. Close the oven door and continue cooking for 10 minutes.

Reduce the oven temperature to 180°/350°F/Gas Mark 4 and continue cooking for about 20 minutes. Check to see if the filling is set right across the tart by gently nudging the tart case. The end result should be set but barely so; it may take a further 10 minutes. Do not overcook, otherwise the texture will be ruined, and remember that the lemon custard will carry on firming up slightly after it has been removed from the oven. Leave to cool for at least 20 minutes.

Scatter a thin layer of caster sugar over the top and torch it! A hot grill will do if you haven't a blowtorch, but protect the pastry round the edge with foil so it doesn't burn.

While the tart is still warm, lift it out on to a serving plate. Don't ruin it with more cream – it needs nothing richer. Having said that, I made a blood orange and cardamom ice cream last winter and served it alongside the tart and the combination was dynamite. The ice cream was a delicate shade of pale pink and no one could guess what it was.

Hazelnut and Apricot Tart

SERVES 6–8

Shortcrust Pastry (see page 158)
225 g/8 oz Hunza apricots, soaked in apple juice, stewed, stoned and puréed
125 g/4 oz butter
4 egg yolks and 3 egg whites
85 g/3 oz vanilla caster sugar
125 g/4 oz ground hazelnuts

If you can't be bothered with soaking and stewing the apricots, use some good apricot jam; this is, after all, a homely variation of Bakewell tart.

Preheat the oven to 220°C/425°F/Gas Mark 7. Roll out the pastry and use to line a 22 cm/9 inch round tart tin. Spread the apricot purée on the pastry.

Melt the butter until it is golden brown. Beat together the eggs and sugar. Stir in the melted butter, then the hazelnuts. If the mixture doesn't feel quite slack enough – it should be dropping consistency – you could whisk in a little single cream. Pour into the pastry case and bake in the oven for 25–30 minutes, until the filling is set. Serve hot or warm.

CHAPTER 6

Christmas in the West

Christmas and New Year in the west of Ireland is a magical time, whatever the weather. No matter if there are howling gales and storms, in between feasting it is mandatory to brave the elements. The informal entertaining becomes slightly more formalized. A telephone call inviting one to supper or to a St Stephen's Day dinner may come a day or two in advance. The great thing is, the children are always included, which is rarely the case in England, and they stay up until the small hours, resurfacing around mid-day. It doesn't seem to matter out here in the dark, short, midwinter days, when the turf fire is banked up and no one is in a hurry to come out from under the bedclothes.

On St Stephen's Day, children from all around go 'on the Wren Boys', disguising themselves and walking and cycling the tracks for miles around, knocking on doors

Looking out to sea from the Mweelrea Mountains.

and singing or playing their tin whistles – or flute in my son Harry's case – until they are given some money. Some are chased until their identity is revealed, and straggles of children of all ages, in groups, twos or on their own, appear at the door until well after dark. Sated with mince pies, sweets, satsumas and the like, pockets weighed down with coins, they come back and count out their loot, the larger children often reaching three-figure sums, the little ones ecstatic to have made £5 or £6.

Our first Christmas here, with a huge free-range turkey from a neighbour, we went next door to our neighbours Tommy and Mary to drink while the turkey roasted, and emerged three hours later in the early afternoon, with me hoping against hope that the fowl hadn't been thoroughly cremated.

I needn't have worried; the cooker had been struggling to keep up to speed, loaded as it was with turkey, separate stuffing, roasting parsnips and potatoes, not a square inch free, and all was perfect.

I have never understood the school of cookery that believes in rising at dawn on Christmas Day to get the turkey into the oven at seven in the morning. Christmas shouldn't be a terrible obstacle course if you make everything you can in advance: cranberry sauce, stuffing, brandy butter, with matured Christmas pudding and mince pies. I always make a fresh orange jelly too, a brilliantly light, tangy ending to the glut of rich, heavy food, and something my mother always did for us when we were children. You can be more adventurous and make it with port, but the simple clear flavour of freshly squozen oranges is unbeatable.

I have made the same stuffing for the turkey for years, and seen no reason to alter it. It is simply the most delicious one I know, that defies experimentation or refinement. Christmas 1995 we spent with my brother Dan in Wicklow, my mother and my friend Tor Belfrage flew out, and we settled in for some serious eating and drinking. I think it was Christmas Eve when my mother confessed that she loathed chestnuts and abhorred walnuts, the two principal ingredients of the famous stuffing. I sped through the Wicklow Mountains on a last-minute dash for the ingredients for Jane Grigson's parsley and lemon stuffing, and decided I'd fill the bird from either end with the two different stuffings. There was enough left of my chestnut recipe to bake a whole dish of it separately, not forgetting the three pints of bread sauce that is a family weakness, and Tor looked on in complete astonishment, thinking I'd gone mad and was catering for the village. My mother was dished up her stuffing. She helped herself liberally to the chestnut one too, until she was warned off it. Undeterred she began . . . and pronounced it utterly delicious. Bizarre. So, if you don't like chestnuts or walnuts, this could still be the best stuffing you ever tasted.

Chestnut Stuffing

3 tbsp olive oil
1 very large onion, finely chopped
½ a head of celery, finely chopped
125 g/4 oz walnuts, finely chopped
2 dessert apples, preferably Cox's, cored but not peeled, finely chopped
1 tin (about 450 g/1 lb) sweet chestnut purée
450 g/1 lb best sausagemeat (I buy organic pork sausagemeat from Swaddles Green Farm see page 109)
about 225 g/8 oz fresh wholemeal breadcrumbs
2 eggs, beaten
2 tbsp finely chopped fresh parsley
salt and pepper
450 g/1 lb vacuum-packed chestnuts

These quantities are enough to fill a large turkey, and for a separate roasting tin covered in foil which you can cook at 190°C/375°F/Gas Mark 5 for a couple of hours. If you can't find vacuum-packed chestnuts, buy 900 g/2 lb of chestnuts in their shells and roast them on the fire or boil them, then shell them.

Heat the oil in a frying pan and gently fry together the onion, celery, walnuts and apples until golden and softened.

Turn into a huge bowl and add all the remaining ingredients, mixing well; add the whole chestnuts last, chopped in four, so they don't break up during mixing.

Use to stuff the bird, and put the remainder in a separate roasting tin.

Roast Turkey with Chestnut Stuffing

3–4 large onions, cut into rings
7 kg/14 lb turkey, with liver and giblets reserved
about 125 g/4 oz butter, softened
sea salt and pepper
about 150 ml/5 fl oz red wine – possibly more

Weigh the bird stuffed, and calculate the cooking time in the following way: 15 minutes for each 450 g/1 lb up to 7 kg/14 lb, so a 7 kg/14 lb bird will take 3½ hours. For each additional 450 g/1 lb over the 7 kg/14 lb bird, allow an extra 10 minutes.

Preheat the oven to 200°C/400°F/Gas Mark 6. Put a layer of onion rings in your roasting tin, and stand the bird on them on its side. Spread the softened butter all over it, with some salt and pepper, and cover the bird with foil that you tuck tightly round the roasting tin so no steam can escape. Cook for 1½ hours, remove the foil, turn the bird on to its other side cover with the foil and roast for a further 1½ hours.

Remove the foil again, turn the bird breast side up, sprinkle with some sea salt to crisp up, and some pepper, and cook for a final 30 minutes or so; you may want to turn the heat up to 230°C/450°F/Gas Mark 8. Remove the bird to a carving dish, cover tightly with foil and lay a clean tea towel on top, then leave to stand for up to 25 minutes so that the juices that have been forced to the centre of the bird by the heat can redistribute themselves through the meat. I do this when roasting anything. As the juice collects, add it to the roasting tin.

Add the giblets and liver to the roasting tin with the caramelized onions, stir well and place over a medium heat. Splash in some red wine and bring the gravy to boiling point. Add the reserved vegetable water from the parboiled parsnips and/or potatoes, and continue boiling so all the flavours can mingle. Pour through a sieve into a jug, having discarded the giblets, but pushing through as much of the liver and onion as you can. The caramelized onions and the red wine will have made the gravy dark, and the intense flavour will need nothing else, certainly not flour or stock cubes.

Crisp Roast Potatoes

Passed down to me, originally I believe from my great grandmother, was the consummate method of crisping roast potatoes. After parboiling and dropping them into the hot fat in the roasting tin – I use olive oil, not dripping – you should ruffle them all over with a fork. An hour later, after turning a couple of times, they are perfect.

Bread Sauce

I like bread sauce with some texture, and find that some types of white breadcrumbs can make it a bit slimy. I prefer this method, with bits of onion, to the more usual one of putting in a whole onion spiked with cloves and removing it at the end of the cooking time.

Finely chop 1 onion and add it to a saucepan with 1.2 litres/ 2 pints of cold milk. Add a good grating of nutmeg, a bay leaf, some black pepper, 3 cloves, and enough fresh wholemeal breadcrumbs to not quite absorb the milk at first. Bring very slowly to simmering point, then stir and simmer for 45 minutes, adding more nutmeg and milk if needed and, if you like, a couple of tablespoons of cream at the end, although I don't think this is necessary. Remove the bay leaf and the cloves if you can find them, season to taste and serve hot.

Christmas Pudding

Makes 2 puddings

200 g/7 oz wholemeal flour
1 tsp mixed spice
1 tsp grated nutmeg
1 tsp ground ginger
275 g/10 oz sultanas
275 g/10 oz currants
200 g/7 oz raisins
200 g/7 oz mixed candied peel, finely chopped
450 g/1 lb dark muscovado sugar
125 g/4 oz blanched almonds, chopped
200 g/7 oz fresh brown breadcrumbs
200 g/7 oz shredded suet
1 large carrot, grated
3 Cox's apples, grated with the skin
6 eggs
300 ml/10 fl oz Guinness
50 ml/2 fl oz brandy
juice and grated rind of 1 orange
milk to mix

As far as I am concerned, the blacker and richer the better, and to this end my Christmas Puddings are pretty Irish, relying on 300 ml/ 10 fl oz of Guinness to help lubricate the fruits and dry ingredients. If you can remember and can face making Christmas pudding in September, do; if not, make it at least six weeks before Christmas Day. By November, the pudding needs 'feeding'. A few skewered holes in the pudding, topped up with brandy, helps mature and marry the flavours. This is a rich but fruity pudding, with the minimum amount of suet. I use a vegetable suet; you can, of course, use ordinary suet.

Grease two 600 ml/1 pint pudding basins. Sift the flour into a large bowl with the mixed spice, nutmeg and ginger. Add the dried fruit and peel, sugar, almonds, breadcrumbs and suet, then the grated carrot and apples.

Beat the eggs well and add the Guinness, whisking until frothy. Then add the brandy, orange juice and rind, and stir into the dry ingredients. Add enough milk to get to a soft, dropping consistency. Divide the mixture between the two basins, cover with greaseproof paper and foil and tie securely with string, then boil for 7 hours.

To store, remove the wrappings and cover with clean greaseproof paper and foil. The puddings will need a further 1½ hours boiling before serving.

Mince Pies with Homemade Mincemeat

Makes 3–4 jars

450 g/1 lb each of currants and raisins
225 g/8 oz sultanas
450 g/1 lb Cox's apples, peeled, cored and finely chopped
450 g/1 lb dark muscovado sugar
200 g/7 oz candied peel, finely chopped
50 g/2 oz each of almonds and pecans, or 125 g/4 oz blanched almonds or walnuts, finely chopped
grated rind and juice of 2 large lemons
grated rind of 1 orange
1 tsp finely grated nutmeg
¼ tsp ground cloves
¼ tsp ground cinnamon
⅛ tsp ground mace
⅛ tsp ground ginger
4 tbsp dark rum
150 ml/5 fl oz brandy

Mincemeat is so much better homemade; it is absurdly quick and easy, and is not something to be lazy about. It is also lovely to have your own jars of mincemeat, to dish out extravagantly to friends around Christmas. When Christmas is over, I invariably have a couple of jars left over, and make a huge old-fashioned lattice mince tart. Experiment with your pastry for mince pies. You could replace half the flour with ground almonds, or add brandy or orange juice instead of the usual water to mix. Grated orange rind is also delicious flecked into the pastry. Almond or walnut oil can be used sparingly as a proportion of the fat – a tablespoon is enough. Making the mincemeat is an annual ritual in our house in late November, with the children measuring, stirring, licking and chopping, and decorating the labels on the jars. You can add suet if you like, but this recipe works brilliantly without it. It should be made at least three weeks before you need it.

Mix all the ingredients together, stirring well, then spoon into clean jars. The mincemeat keeps for months. You can turn the jars upside down every so often to moisten the fruit at the top.

Brandy Butter

SERVES 8–10

225 g/8 oz unsalted butter
125 g/4 oz icing sugar
2–3 tbsp brandy
grated rind of 1 orange
pinch of grated nutmeg
a squeeze of lemon juice

Cut the softened butter into small pieces and cream it in a bowl, using a wooden spoon. Sift the icing sugar over the butter, add the other ingredients and work everything together with your hands. Taste and add more nutmeg and lemon juice if necessary. It keeps well in a covered bowl in the fridge for up to a month.

Fresh Orange Jelly

SERVES 6

juice of ½ a lemon
pared rind of ½ a lemon
pared rind of 1 orange
85 g/3 oz caster sugar
300 ml/10 fl oz water
35 g/1¼ oz powdered gelatine, or the equivalent of leaf gelatine
600 ml/1 pint freshly squeezed orange, clementine or blood orange juice

Put the lemon juice and rind and the orange rind into a saucepan with the sugar and 150 ml/5 fl oz of the water. Place over a low heat and leave to infuse. Soak the gelatine for 10 minutes in the other 150 ml/5 fl oz of water. Add the soaked gelatine (and water) to the saucepan, stir to melt the gelatine, then strain and leave to cool. Add the gelatine liquid to the orange juice, stir well and pour into a decorative jelly mould or glass bowl. Leave to set.

When set, dip the mould very briefly in a basin of scalding water, and turn the jelly out on to a plate. The satisfaction of a perfectly turned out, turreted jelly is as great as the equivalent sandcastle on the beach. You could serve alongside it some orange segments from which you have first removed all the peel and pith, using a very sharp knife. Squeeze some more juice over them and add 1 teaspoon of orange-flower water.

New Year's Eve in the west is another excuse for feasting, before meeting all the neighbours in the bar of the local hotel to see in the New Year. This is when I traditionally cook a goose, and John and Merci come over, and my brother if he's in the country.

Roast Goose with Potato, Sage and Goose Liver Stuffing, and Apple Sauce

The simplest, least-rich stuffing and some plain apple sauce sharpened with orange juice are all that this fattiest and richest of birds needs. The rare occasions one eats goose, I feel the flavour of the bird should stand out; it doesn't need showing off.

SERVES 6–8

450–675 g/1–1½ lb potatoes, depending on the size of the goose
85–125 g/3–4 oz unsalted butter
salt and pepper, grated nutmeg
6–8 onions
12–14 fresh sage leaves
2 tbsp olive oil
4.8–6 kg/10–12 lb goose, with its heart and liver cut into thin strips, discarding any green bits

APPLE SAUCE:
12 Cox's apples
3–4 tbsp unsweetened apple juice
pared rind of 1 orange
juice of ½–1 orange

Preheat the oven to 220°C/450°F/Gas Mark 7. Peel and boil the potatoes, then drain and mash them, or put them through a *mouli-légumes*. Add the butter, salt, pepper and nutmeg to taste.

Chop 3–4 of the onions and cook in boiling water for 10 minutes, then drain and stir into the potato mixture. Tear the sage leaves into small pieces, and stew in the olive oil over a low heat until the scent really comes out of them. Add the goose liver and heart and cook until pink, with the blood still running. Tip the contents of the pan into the potato and onion mixture, stir gently, and stuff the body of the goose.

Slice the remaining onions into rings and place in a layer in your roasting tin. Add the stuffed goose, breast down, and roast for 1–1½ hours. Turn the bird breast side up, scatter with salt and pepper, and roast for a further 1 hour or so, spiking with a thin skewer every 20 minutes. Drain off the fat at intervals and keep it to make the most delicious roast potatoes.

For the apple sauce, simply chop the apples, skins, cores and all, and stew in a tiny amount of apple juice until tender, with the pared orange rind. Rub through a sieve, stir in a little orange juice and leave to cool.

The usual accompaniments of roasted potatoes and parsnips and plainly steamed Brussels sprouts are the best.

Seville Orange and Marmalade Tart

SERVES 6–8

Shortcrust Pastry (see page 158) made with plain white flour
2–3 tbsp tart orange marmalade
grated rind and juice of 4 Seville oranges
125 g/4 oz butter, softened
225 g/8 oz vanilla caster sugar
4 large eggs, beaten

A tangy, fruity pudding, delicious after roast goose. If it is not Seville orange season, use ordinary oranges and less sugar, or one lemon with three oranges.

Preheat the oven to 180°C/350°F/Gas Mark 4. Roll out the pastry and use to line a 22 cm/9 inch tart tin. Bake blind for 15 minutes, then remove the greaseproof paper and beans and bake for a further 5 minutes. Spread the marmalade over the bottom of the tart.

Put the grated orange rind in a bowl. Beat in the butter and sugar, then add the beaten eggs and whisk everything together. Place the bowl over a saucepan of simmering water and stir until the mixture has melted and dissolved. Remove from the heat and stir in the orange juice. Pour over the marmalade-lined tart and return to the oven for 15–20 minutes, or until barely set. Serve warm, with thick cream if you like.

The holy mountain, Croagh Patrick.

CHAPTER 7

Chocolate and Mad March Hares

As a family of unashamed pudding lovers and chocolate lovers, I always thank God that there is no season for chocolate; the deprivation would be almost too awful to contemplate. I have built up a repertoire of favourite puddings, tarts, ice creams and cakes over the years, varying in their degrees of chocolatiness, but alike in that they only taste their best when made with the best chocolate. If I am serving one fruity pudding I usually try and make a chocolate one as well if I am entertaining. If the chocolate pudding is obscenely rich on its own, I make a complementary light one to go alongside it.

David Heneghan on Courtney, Old Head Beach.

Rich Chocolate Fondant

Serves 6–8

150 g/5 oz best bitter chocolate, chopped
150 g/5 oz unsalted butter
1 tbsp brandy
150 ml/5 fl oz warm water
125 g/4 oz caster sugar
4 eggs, separated
25 g/1 oz self-raising flour, sifted

Praline:

25 g/1 oz each of almonds, walnuts and hazelnuts
2 tbsp water
40 g/1½ oz caster sugar
1 tsp unsalted butter
oil for greasing a baking sheet

Optional:

300 ml/10 fl oz double cream
grated chocolate

Unbelievably, this pudding demanded to be made the same New Year's Eve we tucked in to goose and the Seville Orange and Marmalade Tart (see page 124). Somehow we all managed to eat both puddings, and finish them – even the children.

First make the praline. Preheat the oven to 230°C/450°F/Gas Mark 8. Roast the nuts on a baking sheet for 6–8 minutes, then transfer them to a saucepan with the water and sugar and cook for 3–4 minutes until the sugar turns golden brown. Remove from the heat and mix in the butter. Pour the mixture on to a lightly oiled baking sheet, leave to cool and then bash into bits or process roughly – do not grind to crumbs.

Grease a 1.7 litre/3 pint soufflé dish. Turn the oven down to 200°C/400°F/Gas Mark 6. Gently melt the chocolate with the butter and brandy, over a double boiler if you feel safer that way! Add the warm water and sugar, and stir until smooth. Pour the mixture into a bowl. Stir in the egg yolks, then the flour, and beat with a wire whisk until smooth. In a separate bowl, whisk the egg whites until stiff, then gradually incorporate them into the chocolate mixture, folding them in gently with a metal spoon. Pour half the mixture into the soufflé dish, sprinkle the pralined nuts on top, then pour on the remaining mixture. Put the soufflé dish into a deep roasting tin, and pour boiling water into the tin to come halfway up the sides of the soufflé dish. Cook for 10 minutes, then turn the oven down to 160°C/325°F/Gas Mark 3 and continue to cook for about 25 minutes. The pudding should just quake at the centre, but should not feel liquid.

Serve warm, or leave to cool completely. If you are serving it cold, you could whip 300 ml/10 fl oz of double cream until thick but not stiff, and smooth it over the top of the fondant, then finely grate some chocolate over the surface. Moreish!

Frozen Chocolate Parfait

Serves 8

7 egg yolks
125 g/4 oz vanilla caster sugar
200 g/7 oz best bitter chocolate, chopped
1 tbsp amaretto, brandy or strong freshly made black coffee
600 ml/1 pint double cream

A parfait is like a light ice cream, and is best made in a terrine or loaf tin, so you can turn it out and slice it, and serve it with a richly dark chocolate and coffee sauce.

Line a 25 cm/10 inch long terrine or loaf tin with cling film. Whisk the egg yolks with the vanilla caster sugar over a double boiler in a bowl large enough for the ingredients to expand to well over double their original size; this will take 10–15 minutes. The more you beat, the more the eggs expand in volume, and the lighter the result.

In a separate bowl, melt the chocolate with the amaretto, brandy or coffee, then stir it into the egg and sugar mixture. Pour in the cream and whisk until the mixture forms soft peaks. Pour into the lined terrine and freeze until set.

The terrine needs to be dipped into boiling water for a few seconds before turning out on to a plate and peeling away the cling film.

Chocolate Sauce

100 g/3½ oz best bitter chocolate, chopped
25 g/1 oz unsalted butter
2 tbsp freshly made black coffee
few drops of vanilla extract
2–3 tbsp double cream
1 generous tbsp golden syrup

This sauce is wonderful with ice creams, brownies, or Old-Fashioned Steamed Chocolate Pudding (see page 130).

Simply place all the ingredients together in a small saucepan and heat gently until melted and smooth. Serve hot or cold.

Old-Fashioned Steamed Chocolate Pudding

Serves 6–8

125 g/4 oz plain white or wholemeal flour
1 tsp baking powder
125 g/4 oz ground almonds
125 g/4 oz unsalted butter, cut into small pieces
125 g/4 oz caster sugar
25 g/1 oz cocoa
2 eggs, beaten
1–2 tbsp milk
few drops of vanilla extract
100 g/3½ oz best bitter chocolate, grated

Optional:
Chocolate Sauce (see page 129)

Memories of school, when chocolate pudding was made with cocoa only, and the sauce was a kind of bland, watery, lumpy chocolate custard. I like to pour some of the hot chocolate sauce over the pudding when it is turned out, then quickly spike it, hedgehog-like, with blanched roasted almonds. A perfect winter pudding that will guarantee you won't want to move for several hours afterwards. Definitely for months with an 'R' in them, although it wouldn't come amiss on a squally, cold, summer's day in the west of Ireland.

Sift the flour and baking powder into a bowl or into a food processor. Add the ground almonds and the butter and rub in lightly or process to a fine, crumb-like consistency. Add the sugar and cocoa, then the beaten eggs. Add enough milk to give a dropping consistency, and stir in the vanilla and the grated chocolate.

Put the mixture into a greased 1.2 litre/2 pint pudding basin and steam for 1 hour. If you want to, you can serve a homemade custard sauce or single cream alongside the chocolate sauce. Keep half the chocolate sauce back if you are going to anoint and decorate the pudding, and serve it separately in a jug.

Chocolate and Chestnut Terrine

SERVES 8

1 kg/2½ lb vacuum-packed chestnuts
125 g/4 oz unsalted butter, melted
125 g/4 oz vanilla caster sugar
200 g/7 oz best bitter chocolate, chopped
1 tbsp brandy
1 tbsp water

Chocolate and chestnuts is an idyllic combination, and both can be kept in the storecupboard for when you need a delicious and impressive pudding and have run out of fruit or can't be bothered to go shopping. The French cooked, shelled and vacuum-packed chestnuts turn what would be a marathon of a pudding into something instant. The quality is so good you won't notice the difference. With tinned chestnuts you most certainly would.

Put the chestnuts into a food processor with the melted butter and sugar. Blend until evenly mixed.

Melt the chocolate with the brandy and water (I have made this pudding with Irish whiskey when the brandy has run out). Blend this with the chestnut mixture, and put into an oiled 25 cm/10 inch long loaf tin or terrine. Refrigerate overnight, or, if you need it more urgently, put in the freezer for as long as you can. Turn out and serve in thin slices, as it is very rich. Single cream into which you have strained a couple of tablespoons of freshly made coffee is delicious served alongside the terrine.

Wholewheat Chocolate Hazelnut Cake

MAKES AN 18 CM/7 INCH ROUND CAKE

175 g/6 oz unsalted butter
175 g/6 oz light muscovado sugar
3 eggs, beaten
2 tbsp milk
175 g/6 oz wholemeal flour, sifted
2½ tsp baking powder
200 g/7 oz best bitter chocolate, chopped quite small
125 g/4 oz ground hazelnuts
25 g/1 oz chopped hazelnuts

This is a surprisingly subtle and delicious cake, with a melting chocolate and toasted hazelnut top, which my cousin Deborah first cooked for me some years ago. We compulsively swap recipes, and this one I have adapted minutely, by keeping back some of the chocolate to melt in with the hazelnuts on top. It might appear plain – it absolutely isn't.

Preheat the oven to 180°C/350°F/Gas Mark 4. Grease and line an 18 cm/7 inch round cake tin; it should be springform so you can cool the cake without having to turn it upside down.

Cream the butter with the sugar until light and fluffy. Add the eggs, a little at a time, beating between each addition. Then fold in the milk, sifted flour and baking powder, mixing them thoroughly. Add about two-thirds of the chopped chocolate, together with the ground hazelnuts, and spoon the mixture into the prepared tin.

Finally, sprinkle the chopped hazelnuts and the remaining chocolate over the mixture and bake in the centre of the oven for about 1½ hours, or until the centre is springy when lightly touched. After the first hour, cover the cake with a sheet of greaseproof paper to prevent the nuts from burning.

Leave to cool slightly in the tin, then carefully release the springform clip and transfer the cake to a wire rack. Best eaten while still just warm, with or without cream.

Wholewheat chocolate hazelnut cake.

Miranda's Chocolate Birthday Cake

MAKES AN 18 CM/7 INCH ROUND CAKE

175 g/6 oz good dark chocolate, chopped
175 g/6 oz unsalted butter
175 g/6 oz caster sugar
4 eggs, separated
85 g/3 oz ground almonds
85 g/3 oz flour, sifted

RICH CHOCOLATE ICING:
125 g/4 oz good dark chocolate, chopped
40 g/1½ oz butter
50 g/2 oz caster sugar
85 ml/3 fl oz double cream

There is nothing like the first cake your daughter – or son – cooks for you, particularly if it has been made almost secretly for your birthday, and the kitchen, which will have been reduced to rubble, with seemingly every implement used, has also, magically, then been cleaned up. It is even better if the recipe isn't one of those moronic apologies for children's cooking, just as time-consuming and difficult to cook, and disgustingly inedible. This is the wondrously sticky chocolate cake my eldest daughter Miranda cooked for me one birthday. It has become a regular now, and she sweetly cooked it for my mother who had been mourning the loss of birthday cakes one experiences on growing up. A competent nine or ten year old is well up to it.

Preheat the oven to 180°C/350°F/Gas Mark 4. Grease two 18 cm/7 inch sandwich tins or one deeper, 20 cm/8 inch round tin. Melt the chocolate in a bowl over a saucepan of hot water. Cream the butter with the sugar (this is easily done in a food processor), then add the egg yolks one by one, then the almonds, flour and the melted chocolate. Whisk the egg whites until they form soft peaks, then gently fold them into the mixture, little by little.

Divide the mixture between the two sandwich tins and cook in the oven for about 20 minutes. If using one deeper tin, cook for slightly longer. Miranda undercooks hers slightly for a damp, sticky centre. Leave to cool slightly in the tin, then turn out on to a wire rack.

For the icing, put all the ingredients into a bowl over a saucepan of hot water and stir gently over the heat. When smooth, leave to cool and then put into the fridge – it thickens as it cools, and becomes much easier to spread. If you have two sponges, sandwich them together with half the icing and spread half on top. If you have one cake, cover the top and sides copiously with icing.

There is a family of hares living in the field that separates the house from the road, whose habits you could set your watch by with near-perfect accuracy. Their early morning antics take place at the side of the field, near where it adjoins a more rushy, boggy field.

If I am sitting in the sun outside the kitchen door at the back of the house, facing the changing light and cloud of the mountain at late breakfast, the father hare, as I presume him to be, strolls leisurely past me, barely two yards away, up and off to his daytime pursuits. Later on, in the pre-dusk magic hour, the hares return to the field for supper and play, and this they have been doing since I bought the house five years ago. I couldn't possibly consider jugging or roasting these lean, graceful ebullient cohabitants of mine, yet, at Easter, when their heads are turned, there is a humane way!

This spring I finally witnessed evidence of the meaning of the phrase 'mad March hare'. The creatures were chasing their tails, running, jumping and disporting themselves in a state of apparent frenzy. The maddest didn't get away with it. Cycling the coast road in the early morning, John found not one but two at full stretch across the road, dead but still warm, hit but not ruinously, and straddled them across the handlebars before hanging, skinning and paunching them. Some neighbours were horrified we'd picked them off the road, others were eager to come to dinner and try the succulently gamey flavour, offset by a piquant sauce made with the hare liver, heart and blood, garlic, red wine and red wine vinegar.

Bog moss, Co. Mayo.

Civet of Hare with an Aillade

5–6 tbsp olive oil
2 onions, chopped
6 carrots, cut into long sticks
3 sticks of celery, chopped
3 cloves garlic, chopped
1 hare, jointed
2–3 tbsp plain flour
300 ml/10 fl oz red wine
1 tbsp tomato purée
2 squares of bitter chocolate
1 bouquet garni with 3 bay leaves, 2 sprigs of rosemary, parsley and thyme, tied together with string
salt and pepper
5–6 juniper berries
a little stock (hare, beef or chicken)
225 g/8 oz mushrooms, sliced

AILLADE:
12–14 cloves garlic, finely chopped
1 small onion, finely chopped
175 g/6 oz unsmoked streaky bacon, finely chopped
liver and heart of the hare, finely chopped
blood of the hare
85 ml/3 fl oz red wine vinegar
85–150 ml/3–5 fl oz red wine
salt and pepper

I allow four people to a hare: the saddle halved and two back legs. The small front legs can be used for second helpings and the rib-cage for stock.

Preheat the oven to 150°C/300°F/Gas Mark 2. Heat 3 tablespoons of the olive oil and sauté the onions, carrots, celery and garlic in a casserole until softened. Remove from the casserole with a slotted spoon and put on a plate. Add some more olive oil to the casserole, roll the hare joints lightly in flour and brown them briefly all over. Return the sautéd vegetables to the casserole, then add the red wine, the tomato purée and the chocolate. Tuck in the bouquet garni, add the seasonings and juniper berries and a ladle of stock, bring it to boiling point, then cover and cook in a slow oven for 1½–2 hours. The hare should be beginning to fall off the bone. Half an hour before eating, sauté the sliced mushrooms briefly in olive oil, then add to the casserole.

While the hare is cooking, make the *aillade*. Put all the ingredients in a small saucepan with 85 ml/3 fl oz of the wine, season with salt and pepper, and simmer very gently for 1½ hours. If the liquid is drying up, splash in some more red wine.

When you dish up each portion of hare and vegetables, put a tablespoon of *aillade* on top, and serve with redcurrant jelly. Very good with a potato and celeriac purée, made with two-thirds potatoes to one-third celeriac. Steam the chopped celeriac, boil the potatoes, and mash together with butter, salt, pepper and grated nutmeg. It can also be accompanied with a Gratin of Brussels Sprouts or Baked Beetroot with Sour Cream.

Gratin of Brussels Sprouts

Parboil the sprouts for 3–4 minutes, drain them, chop roughly, and put them in a buttered gratin dish. Pour 150–300 ml/5–10 fl oz of double cream over them, season with salt, pepper and grated nutmeg, sprinkle a handful of brown breadcrumbs over the surface, and dot with small knobs of butter. Bake for about 20–25 minutes at 200°C/400°F/Gas Mark 6.

Baked Beetroot with Sour Cream

This dish is particularly good with the strong, gamey flavour of hare, venison or grouse. Use smallish beetroots which you have scrubbed but not peeled. Cook them as you would a baked potato, on a baking sheet in the oven: the flavour is much more intense if they are baked rather than boiled. They will take at least 2 hours in a slow oven, 150°C/300°F/Gas Mark 2. When they are tender, peel and slice them, and put them in a shallow serving dish. Pour some heated sour cream over them, into which you have finely chopped some chives – or dill if they are to accompany fish – and salt and pepper.

Rabbits have returned to our stretch of coast. There are arteries of burrows in the more sheltered, permanent dunes, others in the fields and hedgerows. Neighbours at the end of our track whose house perches above dunes, beach and sea, isolated and unfrequented, swear that the rabbits are so unused to the sight or sound of a gun that if they shoot one as it frolics in the early evening, the others don't even dive for cover, but remain hopelessly unaware that they could be the next target. A veritable pot shot. I have never minded the lurking shrapnel, the shards of splintery bone; a good rabbit casserole suffused with thyme and warmed with mustard is a classic – hearty, meaty and not too rich for the delicately flavoured flesh. Tame rabbit is another story – the flavour is simply not there.

Rabbit Stewed with Thyme in a Mustard Sauce

Serves 6

1 wild rabbit, jointed
2–3 tbsp plain flour
salt and pepper
4–5 tbsp olive oil
675 g/1½ lb belly pork, cubed
3 carrots, quartered
1 large onion, chopped
3–4 sticks of celery, roughly chopped
6 cloves garlic, peeled but left whole
1 bouquet garni with 3 bay leaves, 3 good sprigs of parsley and a handful of thyme, tied together with string
300 ml/10 fl oz dry white wine or dry cider
300 ml/10 fl oz rabbit or chicken stock
3 egg yolks
175 ml/6 fl oz double cream
1 tbsp English mustard
1 tbsp coarse grain mustard

Optional:
1 tsp finely chopped fresh thyme

Toss the rabbit joints in seasoned flour, and brown them lightly in a casserole with 2–3 tablespoons of the oil and the cubed belly pork. Remove from the casserole with a slotted spoon and put on a plate. Add some more oil to the casserole and gently sauté the carrots, onion, celery and garlic. Return the meat to the casserole and tuck in the bouquet garni. Add the wine or cider and stock, bring to a simmer, cover tightly and simmer gently or bake in a slow oven, 150°C/300°F/Gas Mark 2, for 1–2 hours. Check after an hour; the meat should be very tender. Pour all the liquid from the casserole through a sieve into a jug, and replace the lid immediately to keep the rabbit hot.

In a bowl, beat together the egg yolks, cream, and both mustards. Whisk in a ladleful of the hot rabbit cooking liquid, then whisk in the remainder and pour into a small saucepan. Heat very gently to avoid curdling; do not let it boil. If you like, add a teaspoon of finely chopped fresh thyme, and pour the sauce over the rabbit.

Mashed potatoes, some plainly steamed celery and Carrots Vichy (see page 89) are the only accompaniments you need.

Purple heather by the roadside.

CHAPTER 8

Inish Turk and Favourite Food

Mick O'Toole, a fisherman on Inish Turk, has brought us to the island on his boat for several years now. We have got to know him and his family, and trips to the island have always stood out in my memory. There was the year Mick and his wife Pauline brought their oldest child over to the mainland to start secondary school – there isn't one on the island. Everyone was in tears on the quay, and we were going back to the island with Mick that day. The family was being split up for the first time, and in the winter months bad weather can sometimes prevent boats coming in and out for weeks, leaving children cut off from home.

In late August another summer, after walking the old bog road across the island to the dizzily high cliffs at the far end, the seagulls wheeling slowly beneath us, we returned in fine style with music all the way home. Michael Longley, the poet, who spends a lot of time staying locally and

Aoife Jennings.

writing about Mayo, was in our party. My younger daughter, Charissa, watched with fascination as he lowered himself on to Mick's fishing nets for the return journey, a bottle of whiskey in a brown paper bag in hand to pass round. At the last moment Tim, one of our local butchers, who had been playing music for the islanders the night before – and hadn't been to bed – asked if there was any extra space. He and his girlfriend, a fine flautist, climbed aboard, their trip home guaranteed if they provided the music. With Tim's bowron, the flute, the guitar and our singing we set off through the swirling currents at the back of Caher Island, on a trip that none of us wanted to end, suspended in time and motion, sun and sea, music and Jameson!

Last summer, the hottest and sultriest I remember, Merci Kilcoyne and I decided to go alone, and spend the night. Mick was bringing in a guitarist friend to play that night, so we set off for the island across a glassy, topaz sea, a huge cloudless skyscape behind us. At the tiny harbour we were met by more O'Tooles – the island is inhabited almost entirely by them – and an extraordinary Landrover that looked worthier of a car cemetery than an MOT test. Clearly a chauffeur service was provided to Paddy and Ann's B & B. 'Welcome to Alcatraz,' said our driver, as the panel representing a door was kicked into place, and Merci and I, giggling like children setting off for school, surveyed the hole beneath our feet where a floor should have been. 'Why Alcatraz?' 'Because once you're inside you can't get out.' That was enough to set the tone for our adventure, our Big Girls' night out.

After a convivial tea with the family, Merci and I walked down the track to the community centre where the dancing and drinking were getting under way. By two or three in the morning we decided to get some air and walk down to the quay. There is a curious quietness on small islands, by day and by night, an otherworldliness, a deep-down sense of place and peace. Through the hushed quiet we walked, a murmur of sea, a faint voice, a whisper of song from above, all our senses heightened and alive with the awareness of trespassing on someone's territory yet being welcomed and absorbed. We stumbled through the extraordinary warm reaches of early, early morning to the shebeen, the name for what have traditionally been illicit drinking dens in Ireland. This one had been the only bar until the community centre was built a few years ago. There it felt like the night had only just begun. In a tiny room a party had begun to close in on itself, some traditional musicians had come in from Galway and, grouped around a table, were beginning to fill the place and make it dance attendance. Out in the tiny courtyard a game was going on. How far could a bottle be pushed on the ground and picked up one-handed without the players bending their legs and falling flat on their faces. We joined the contestants. Then we found a couple to dance half a set with and, elated, danced until four or five in the morning, when we padded back up to the O'Tooles', who were still up talking to our musician friend Thomas, realizing that sleep was unlikely.

Later, a proper Irish breakfast, then a walk to the tiny church for Mass, the islanders settling into the weekly ritual as sleeplorn as us, before crossing the sea back home.

This summer it wasn't to be. The first weekend we were booked in with Mick the weather was inclement, the second weekend Mick's 89-year-old mother had died, and the third weekend John K's mother had been taken ill and has also sadly since died.

In the meanwhile we spent a magical day on the mussel co-operative's pilot boat with John and Merci and the children, slipping into the Killary from Bundorragha to the mussel rafts on the far side, where we hauled up three sacks' worth for ourselves and some local restaurants. We brought with us some sea urchins that John had been growing experimentally, and some thick slices of Vincent and Anne Bourke's smoked wild salmon, and Merci's soda bread. By the time we had landed on a little uninhabited island just outside Killary Bay, Inis Jaegel, we were ravenous. Basking seals slid away as we shinned up the seaweed-strewn rocks to the grass above – until we realized there was a plague of ticks. We dived back down to the rocks again, and John knifed open the sea urchins to eat with a teaspoon raw from their shells. Tiny mounds of delicate, softly pink flesh in a clear salty juice, warmed slightly by the sun, a dish of simple perfection. Harry, always ready to try something new, who mopped up a dozen snails as a toddler, was as excited as we were by this new delicacy, savouring the place and the taste equally.

The summer's most prevalent theme was curry. All three children took to exotically spiced dishes with unexpected enthusiasm and delight. Spiced leg of lamb, chicken with ginger and yoghurt, lamb with paprika, prawns in a spicy brown sauce; even the vegetables were eaten with gusto: dal, potatoes with garlic and ginger, cauliflower with roasted cumin, cabbage simmered with green chillies and turmeric.

Chicken in a Ginger and Yoghurt Paste

SERVES 8

1 large chicken, about 1.8 kg/4 lb
3 onions, chopped
a piece of fresh ginger, cut into five 2.5 cm/1 inch cubes, then peeled and chopped
12 cloves garlic, roughly chopped
2–3 green chillies, seeded and finely chopped
50 g/2 oz blanched almonds, roughly chopped
500–600 ml/16–20 fl oz live natural yoghurt
1 tbsp ground cumin
1 tbsp ground coriander seeds
½ tsp cayenne pepper
1 tsp seeds from cardamom pods
1 tsp garam masala
1 tsp salt
3 tbsp olive oil
4–5 cloves
a cinnamon stick
4–5 peppercorns
a handful each of sultanas and flaked almonds
fresh coriander, chopped

This is one of my most successful dishes – chicken or lamb anointed in a thick yoghurt and ginger paste, then roasted with spices after marinating it for 24 hours, and in the case of a dinner delayed by neighbours who were finishing silaging, for 48 hours. It is best to use a large, deep Pyrex dish or an enamelled casserole dish, so that you can marinate and cook the chicken in the same dish. A roasting tin is not suitable for marinating.

Cut the chicken into eight pieces, discarding the skin. Put the onions, ginger, garlic, chillies, blanched almonds and a third of the yoghurt in a food processor and blend to make a smoothish paste. Pour the rest of the yoghurt into a bowl, add the onion paste, cumin, ground coriander, cayenne, cardamom, garam masala and salt and whisk lightly to amalgamate.

Make slashes in the chicken flesh and push in as much of the spicy paste as you can, then pour all the remaining paste over the pieces of chicken. Cover the dish with cling film and refrigerate for, ideally, 24 hours.

Take the dish out of the fridge an hour or so before you intend to cook it. Preheat the oven to 190°C/375°F/Gas Mark 5. Heat the oil in a small frying pan, and when hot drop in the cloves, cinnamon and peppercorns, then pour the whole lot over the chicken.

Cover the dish with foil or a lid and bake for about 30 minutes. Remove the lid, sprinkle on the sultanas and flaked almonds, and put back into the oven, uncovered, for 10 minutes. Test that the chicken is cooked – it might need a few more minutes if the legs are huge. Sprinkle with chopped coriander and serve with rice and poppadums and one or two vegetables such as the ones that follow. A real feast of a dish, not too highly spiced for children.

Cauliflower with Roasted Cumin

SERVES 8 AS AN ACCOMPANIMENT

3 tbsp olive oil
1 tbsp cumin seeds
1 tbsp black mustard seeds
1 tsp fennel seeds
1 large cauliflower, broken into florets
½ tsp each of ground cumin, coriander and turmeric
1 green chilli, seeded and chopped
salt and pepper
pinch of cayenne pepper

OPTIONAL:
potatoes, cooked and cubed
a handful of peas, cooked

This is a dry dish, and therefore a good accompaniment to the thickly sauced chicken. You can include cooked, cubed potatoes if you like, and throw in a handful of peas you have cooked separately at the last minute to add some colour.

Heat the oil in a large frying pan, and when hot add the cumin, mustard and fennel seeds. Let them sizzle for a few seconds before putting in the cauliflower and stirring it to coat. Cover, turn the heat down, and simmer for 5 minutes. The cauliflower will still be crisp. Add the ground cumin, coriander, turmeric and chilli, and season to taste with salt, pepper and cayenne. Stir well.

If you are adding potatoes and peas, put them in at this stage. Cook, uncovered, over a low heat, turning gently until the potatoes are thoroughly heated through and the cauliflower is cooked, up to 5 minutes.

Cabbage with Green Chillies and Turmeric

Serves 8
as an accompaniment

3 tbsp olive oil
1 tsp ground cumin
2 bay leaves
1 small onion, finely chopped
2 cloves garlic, finely chopped
1 white cabbage, cored and shredded
½ tsp turmeric
pinch of cayenne pepper
1 green chilli, seeded and finely chopped
1 tsp light muscovado or caster sugar
1 tsp each of salt and pepper
½ tsp garam masala

Heat the oil in a wide saucepan, then throw in the cumin, bay leaves, onion and garlic; 10 seconds later, add the cabbage. Stir briskly to coat in oil, then add the turmeric and cayenne. Cover, turn the heat right down, and cook for about 5 minutes. Add the chilli, sugar, salt and pepper, stir, cover again and cook for a further 3–4 minutes. Sprinkle the garam masala over the cabbage, stir and serve.

Dal

Serves 8 as an accompaniment

225 g/8 oz Puy lentils, washed
2 slices of fresh ginger
1 tsp turmeric
½ tsp garam masala
1 tsp ground cumin
salt and pepper
2 tbsp olive oil
½ tsp cumin seeds
2 cloves garlic, finely chopped
1 green chilli, seeded, finely chopped

Optional:
spinach, cooked and finely chopped

There are, I am sure, a million ways to cook dal – I like to use the little speckledy Puy lentils, and sometimes add some finely chopped cooked spinach at the end. If you have not added the spinach, leftover dal is delicious as a cold salad, with additional olive oil and some chopped fresh coriander.

Put the lentils into a large saucepan with 1.2 litres/2 pints of cold water and bring to the boil. Add the ginger and turmeric and simmer until tender; this will take about 40 minutes to 1 hour and the water will be very nearly absorbed. Add the garam masala and ground cumin, season to taste and stir. If you are adding spinach, stir it in 3–4 minutes before you finish the dal. You can purée a third of the dal mixture and stir it into the rest if you prefer the texture slightly mushy.

In a separate small frying pan, heat the oil, then throw in the cumin seeds, garlic and chilli and brown them lightly. Pour over the dal before serving.

Cooking for children is rather like the pro-nuclear 'power expands into a vacuum' theory. However big the hole, you can never fill it – for long. Then there is the fact that fads and favourites rotate and change constantly, and one rarely conjures up a dish that gets wholehearted approval from everyone. Boredom is their strongest suit. I still get reminded by Miranda that the reason she doesn't like macaroni cheese is because we once had a nanny who fed it to her twice a week. I know this isn't true, but it doesn't alter the fact that she still can't even look at it, even if the béchamel is cheeseless, and the grated Parmesan she loves is gratinéd to a heavenly crust on top. It is still cheese sauce!

Where I am lucky is that despite their different dislikes, all three are dedicated experimenters and triers. Bland nursery food was never the only answer. Miranda at 18 months used to sit up in bed with me eating homemade garlicky taramasalata for breakfast, insisting that that was the only thing in the world she wanted.

Tentative introductions to Indian and Chinese food have been passionately approved, but there is always one proviso. Certain of their friends are deeply resistant to our 'funny food', so the children beg for normality, for shop-bought pizzas that will not single them out as the possessors of weird parents. Without complying completely, I have taken these strictures as a challenge, to provide delicious, nourishing food that doesn't scream 'healthy', and that meets both junior and senior approval. Terribly important in Ireland, where we are all eating together as a family every day, not at different sittings as we do during term-time. Stews and shepherd's pies are unbeatable family fodder if lovingly and inventively cooked with the best ingredients. Everyday food can be taken out of the realm of the commonplace with a small serving of imagination.

The following are all dishes that I hope people will try on their families when they have got to the furthest, despairing stages: 'what shall I cook today, what can I do that is different – but the same?'

Mozzarella-Stuffed Meatballs with Fresh Tomato Sauce

SERVES 4–6

1 onion
2 cloves garlic
some fresh flat-leaf parsley
450 g/1 lb minced meat
1 tsp chopped thyme or marjoram
salt and pepper
1 egg, beaten
half a buffalo mozzarella, cut into 1 cm/½ inch cubes
flour
6–7 tbsp olive oil

Use the best minced beef or lamb you can afford, or minced steak for a treat.

Mince the onion, garlic and parsley together in a liquidizer or food processor, then add them to the meat in a large bowl. Sprinkle in the chopped fresh thyme or marjoram, some salt and pepper, and then work in the beaten egg with your fingers or a wooden spoon. Roll into balls the size of an extra-large marble, pushing a cube of mozzarella into the centre of each. Roll very lightly in flour, and cook in a large frying pan in a generous amount of olive oil, turning to brown all over. Remove from the pan to a warmed gratin dish, and pour over a quantity of Fresh Tomato Sauce (see opposite). Serve with spaghetti.

Raw Tomato Sauce

SERVES 4

1 small onion
1 large clove garlic
675 g/1½ lb ripe, well-flavoured tomatoes, skinned, seeded and finely chopped
6 tbsp olive oil
1 tbsp each of torn basil leaves, chopped chives and flat-leaf parsley
2 tbsp lemon juice
salt and pepper

This is a family favourite, not, as you might imagine, only in the summer months when it can be tossed into pasta and eaten warm or cold. In the winter we eat it with hot pasta, and it is fresh, healthy and invigorating. The best pasta to serve it with is of the short, squat variety, say a fusilli or chunky macaroni.

Mince the onion and garlic together in a liquidizer or food processor. Put in a bowl with the remaining ingredients, stir, then cover and leave in the fridge for about 30 minutes. Stir again, then stir into a steaming hot bowl of pasta, and serve warm or cold.

Fresh Tomato Sauce

Serves 6 or more

3 tbsp olive oil
2 onions, finely chopped
2 sticks of celery, finely chopped
6 cloves garlic, finely chopped
1 kg/2½ lb Italian plum tomatoes, skinned, seeded and chopped, otherwise the best tomatoes you can get
1 can (400 g/14 oz) Italian plum tomatoes
½ jar (200 g/7 oz) tomato passata, organic if possible
1 tbsp tomato purée
2 bay leaves, generous bunch of fresh thyme, parsley and/or basil
2 tsp molasses sugar
about 150 ml/5 fl oz red wine
salt and pepper

This is the most versatile sauce our family eats, and so far has not been consigned to the realms of the unacceptable. Rather like a lemon tart or a Bolognese sauce, everyone develops their own version of tomato sauce, changing it subtly according to the dish it is going to accompany, the herbs available, the quality of the tomatoes and the desired texture. It is freezable, but if I make a large quantity I generally keep my extra in the fridge to adapt or use a few days later.

Heat the oil in a large, heavy-bottomed frying pan and sauté the onions, celery and garlic until softened and translucent. Add the fresh and canned tomatoes, tomato passata and purée, and chop the canned tomatoes down into the liquid. Add the bay leaves, thyme or parsley, simmer for a minute, then stir in the sugar. Simmer, uncovered, until the sauce is beginning to thicken, stirring occasionally, for about 15 minutes. Add a good splash of wine, season and stir. Keep the sauce simmering happily for up to another 30 minutes, giving it the occasional stir and adding a little more wine or tomato passata if it begins to dry out.

You are now ready to use it plain with pasta, or with the meatballs opposite, scattering some torn basil leaves over the top. Alternatively pour it over some fish – cod is delicious like this – and bake in the oven, or, for a more refined sauce, put it through the *mouli-légumes*. If you fancy something spicier, you can then add harissa to taste, a few pounded anchovies, some black olives and capers, and you have the famously libidinous-sounding tart's pasta, or *pasta puttanesca*.

This summer Vincent Bourke tried to persuade me to buy some pollack he had experimentally smoked. I resisted, thoughts of tweezers and bones unspoken. He handed me the parcel anyway and told me to go off and try it. It made the basis of a succulently delicious kedgeree, in place of the more usual smoked haddock. Proper smoking is the key, naturally; chemically dyed fish is not an option.

Mildly Curried Kedgeree

SERVES 6

675 g/1½ lb oak-smoked haddock or pollack fillets
about 300 ml/10 fl oz milk
a little butter
pepper
325–450 g/12 oz–1 lb brown basmati rice
4 tbsp olive oil
2 large onions, thinly sliced
1 clove garlic, chopped
9–12 eggs
225 g/8 oz fresh or frozen peas
2–3 tbsp double cream (optional)
1 tsp garam masala
a large bunch of parsley, finely chopped

A classic comfort food, needing no accompaniment, no tinkering with, no apologies for. Extraordinary that it shares the rare ranks of dishes that work as well at breakfast as they do at lunch as they do at supper. I suppose the best breakfast food naturally does: kidneys, eggs and bacon, the salmon fishcakes that I used to watch my grandfather eat for breakfast – we were not allowed to share in this indulgence. Champagne is undoubtedly the liquid equivalent, uplifting to the spirits be it at 8 am or 8 pm.

Put a large saucepan of water on to boil. Preheat the oven to 180°C/350°F/Gas Mark 4. Lay the fish in a gratin dish, pour over enough milk to just cover, dot with butter, scrunch over some black pepper and put in the oven for 15 minutes, until just tender. Throw the rice into a saucepan of boiling water, stir, put the lid on, and cook until tender; brown basmati rice takes about 35–40 minutes.

Heat the oil in a large, heavy-bottomed frying pan. Add the onions and garlic and cook over a low heat, stirring for 2–3 minutes, then cover with a lid and stew for about 20 minutes.

When the fish is ready, flake it into decent-sized pieces, removing the bones and skin, and reserve the poaching milk. Drain the rice thoroughly and stir it into the onion and garlic mixture. Gently stir in the fish and add the poaching milk.

Boil the eggs for 6 minutes – they should be neither hard nor runny for this dish. Shell them and halve them. Cook the peas and add them to the kedgeree mixture. Add the cream if you like, and the garam masala, and mix. Turn out on to a large, warmed serving plate and arrange the halved eggs around it. Sprinkle over the parsley and dot with a few knobs of butter. Serve with quartered lemons and mango chutney if you like.

Smoked Haddock and Watercress Tart

Serves 6

325 g/12 oz smoked haddock
300 ml/10 fl oz creamy milk
25 g/1 oz butter
1 small onion, finely chopped
1 stick of celery, finely chopped
25 g/1 oz plain flour
salt and pepper
grated nutmeg
a bunch of watercress, finely chopped
2 eggs, beaten
Shortcrust Pastry (see page 158), baked blind in a 22 cm/9 inch round tin with a removable base
2 tbsp grated Parmesan cheese

This is a more unusual way of using smoked haddock which seems to have as much of an affinity with the peppery, iron-rich leaves of watercress as it does with spinach.

Preheat the oven to 190°C/375°F/Gas Mark 5. Put the haddock and milk in a saucepan and bring to the boil, then reduce tne heat and simmer very gently for 10 minutes. Skin the fish and flake it into a bowl. Reserve the poaching milk.

Heat the butter in a saucepan, add the onion and celery and cook until softened. Stir in the flour and cook for a couple of minutes, then add the reserved poaching milk and stir until the sauce has thickened. Season to taste with salt, pepper and nutmeg. Remove from the heat and stir into the fish, adding the watercress and beaten eggs. Pour into the pastry case and sprinkle the top with Parmesan. Bake in the oven for 25–30 minutes, when the tart will be risen and crusted with golden brown. Leave to cool slightly and turn out on to a plate. Serve with Provençale Tomato Salad (see page 87); the gutsy combination of walnuts and basil works beautifully with the smoked fish and watercress.

Thanks to the Westport country market I can buy a wonderful selection of organically grown herbs every week in the west, beautifully fresh and pungent. Chervil, dill, coriander, chives, flat-leaf parsley, basil, thyme, marjoram and oregano, tarragon and fennel. Most wouldn't grow on the bit of the coast where I am, salt-ridden and starkly unsheltered, so it is a small extravagance. When the fridge is nearly bare at the end of the week, I can still muster a near-complete herb garden.

Strangely, the herbs that one would use on their own with meat or fish work beautifully in combination if herbs are the dominant ingredient. They are well able to preserve their individual strength and flavour, for example in a mixed herb tart, where the herbs are offset by a rich, creamy custard. You can experiment, but the combination that pleased me the most was the following.

Herb Tart

Serves 6

25 g/1 oz butter
1 heaped tbsp each of chopped fresh parsley, tarragon, basil, chives
2 tbsp chopped fresh thyme
2 eggs and 2 egg yolks
450 ml/15 fl oz double cream, or half cream, half milk
salt and pepper
pinch of grated nutmeg
125 g/4 oz Gruyère or Emmental cheese, grated
Shortcrust Pastry (see page 158), baked blind in a 22 cm/9 inch round tin with a removable base
Optional:
1 tbsp grated Parmesan cheese

Preheat the oven to 190°C/375°F/Gas Mark 5. Heat the butter in a heavy-bottomed frying pan, add the herbs and stir briefly to coat. In a large bowl, whisk together the eggs, yolks and cream, season with salt, pepper and nutmeg, then stir in the grated Gruyère or Emmental. Stir in the herbs, then ladle the mixture into the pastry case.

Cook in the oven for about 25 minutes. After about 15 minutes, you can sprinkle on the Parmesan if you want a cheesier flavour. The result should be puffed up and browned. Serve hot or warm.

Prawn and Leek Lasagne

SERVES 6

50 g/2 oz butter or 4 tbsp olive oil
white parts of 12 thick leeks, chopped into 1 cm/½ inch chunks
600 g/1¼ lb lasagne sheets
900 g/2 lb cooked peeled prawns
125–175 g/4–6 oz Parmesan cheese, grated

BÉCHAMEL SAUCE:
900 ml/1½ pints milk
1 bay leaf
1 onion, halved
grated nutmeg
50 g/2 oz butter
50 g/2 oz plain white flour
salt and pepper

Seafood lasagne is a glorious dish, especially with a combination of shellfish – prawns, lobster, clams and mussels – and a firm white fish. This is an everyday version. You can add chunks of skinned, seeded tomato if you like, but in this case I think the excellence is in the simplicity.

First make the béchamel sauce: put the milk in a saucepan with the bay leaf, onion and a generous pinch of nutmeg. Bring to just below boiling point, then remove from the heat and leave to infuse for 15–20 minutes. Melt the butter in a saucepan, stir in the flour and cook, stirring, for 1 minute. Stir the milk and gradually stir it into the flour mixture to make a thick smooth sauce. Season to taste.

Preheat the oven to 190°C/375°F/Gas Mark 5. Heat the butter or oil in a large saucepan, add the leeks and cook over a low heat until softened and translucent.

Boil the lasagne until tender, then drain by spreading the pasta sheets on a clean tea towel. (Alternatively, use the sort of lasagne that does not need precooking.)

Put a thin layer of béchamel sauce in a large greased baking dish and sprinkle about a third of the grated Parmesan on top. Add a layer of lasagne, and scatter half the leeks and half the prawns on top. Pour over half the remaining béchamel and sprinkle another third of the grated Parmesan on top. Repeat the layers, starting with the lasagne and ending with the Parmesan. Cook in the preheated oven for 30–40 minutes. Test by inserting a knife into the pasta; the top will be golden and bubbling.

Serve with a green salad with some finely sliced fennel.

Herb tart.

Pasta in a Chicken Liver Sauce

SERVES 4

450 g/1 lb chicken livers
2–3 tbsp olive oil
2 onions, thinly sliced
2 cloves garlic, finely chopped
450 g/1 lb spaghetti
6–7 sage leaves, finely chopped
2 tbsp balsamic vinegar
4–5 tbsp red or dry white wine
about 150 ml/5 fl oz chicken stock
225 g/8 oz fresh or frozen peas, cooked
salt and pepper

The country market where I get all my herbs, sells properly reared chickens if you order them. The first time I picked up my order, I realized too late that they had come without their livers and giblets, a must for the gravy. The following Thursday I went back. The result, a bag of livers and giblets is saved for me each week – clearly I am the only person for miles around who is desperate for awful offal! Consequently, I have been experimenting with chicken liver parfaits and sauces, and this is a recipe I came up with this summer. It is a dark and intensely flavoured sauce coating juicily pink chunks of chicken livers, which goes particularly well with the nutty taste of buckwheat spaghetti.

Some people advocate soaking the livers in milk for a few hours, but I have not detected a superior result, so I don't bother. Carefully remove all the gristle, fat and any green bits and cut the livers into 1 cm/½ inch wide strips.

Heat the oil in a large, heavy-bottomed frying pan. Add the onions and garlic and sauté gently, then cover and continue cooking over a low heat for about 20 minutes.

Meanwhile, cook the pasta in plenty of boiling water until *al dente* (just tender to the bite).

Add the chicken livers and sage leaves to the pan with the onions and cook briefly to seal the livers, then add the balsamic vinegar and stir well, scraping up the little bits from the bottom of the pan. Add a good splash of wine and a couple of ladles of stock, and bring to a bubble, letting it start to reduce. Add the cooked peas and seasoning, and, as soon as the livers are just cooked, pink in the middle, toss the contents of the pan over the pasta.

Lentil, tomato and pasta soup.

Lentil, Tomato and Pasta Soup

SERVES 6

3 tbsp olive oil
2 onions, finely chopped
6 cloves garlic, finely chopped
2 sticks of celery, finely chopped
125 g/4 oz smoked streaky bacon, chopped small
225 g/8 oz Puy lentils
4 tomatoes, skinned, seeded and chopped
400 g/14 oz can Italian plum tomatoes
about 1.7 litres/3 pints chicken stock
3–4 sprigs of thyme
2 bay leaves
225 g/8 oz macaroni or similar small pasta
salt and pepper
2–3 tbsp chopped fresh parsley
85–125 g/3–4 oz Parmesan cheese, grated

There are soups that are soups, and soups that are stews, complete and nourishing meals in their own right, and a pleasure to the cook who can produce them out of a single pot. This is one of them and one I never tire of, winter or summer. The only accompaniment it needs is garlic bread.

Heat the oil in a large, heavy-bottomed casserole, add the onions, garlic, celery and bacon and cook over a low heat until the vegetables are softened and translucent, about 10–15 minutes. Add the lentils and stir to coat them in oil. Add the fresh and canned tomatoes, chopping the canned ones into their juice. Bring to a bubble, then add the stock, thyme and bay leaves. Bring to the boil, then cover and simmer until the lentils are cooked, about 40 minutes. If the mixture is absorbing a lot of stock, ladle in some more, keeping the level above the lentils.

Cook the pasta in boiling water, drain and add to the soup with an extra couple of ladles of stock. Season well, and sprinkle with parsley. Serve in bowls, sprinkled with the Parmesan.

Soupe au Pistou

SERVES 8–10

225 g/8 oz dried cannellini or haricot beans, soaked overnight
4–5 tbsp olive oil
1 large onion, chopped
2.3–3 litres/4–5 pints chicken stock or water
225 g/8 oz potatoes, cubed
225 g/8 oz carrots, cut into small cubes
1 fat leek, chopped
2 sticks of celery, chopped
salt and pepper
225 g/8 oz string beans, sliced
225 g/8 oz courgettes, chopped
450 g/1 lb tomatoes, skinned, seeded and chopped
50 g/2 oz macaroni
large pinch of saffron threads

PISTOU:
6 cloves garlic, finely chopped
a large handful of fresh basil
2 tbsp grated Parmesan cheese
2 tbsp tomato purée
6 tbsp olive oil

A delicious dish that we first ate as a family in the tiny village of Murs in Provence. Harry, aged 18 months, tucked into it, and demanded bowls of it on each successive trip. A meal in itself.

Drain and rinse the beans and put them in a saucepan with water to cover. Bring to the boil, cover and simmer until tender, 1–1½ hours.

Heat the oil in a large, heavy-bottomed casserole, add the onion and cook over a low heat until softened. Add the stock or water and bring to the boil. Add the potatoes, carrots, leek and celery, and some salt and pepper, and simmer together for about 15 minutes. Stir in the cooked dried beans in their cooking liquid, and add the string beans, courgettes, tomatoes, macaroni and saffron. Simmer until tender, about another 15 minutes.

Meanwhile, make the pistou. Put all the ingredients into a food processor or liquidizer and swirl together. Add a ladleful of the soup liquid to the pistou, stir, and pour it into the soup.

Serve with a bowl of freshly grated Parmesan.

As I have got nearer to completing this book, one thing has got stuck in my mind. Writing, at the beginning, of Old Head days and Mrs Wallace's puddings, I was only able to include two of the three that had imprinted themselves on our collective family memory. The third, inexplicably called Canadian Pie, I had been unable to trace. It had been my father and my brother Daniel's favourite. Even the memory of the taste wasn't enough for me to risk attempting it, although my mother reminded me that my father had adored currants. Finally, this week, after scouring every curranted recipe I could, I found something called Cumberland Tart, which, although it was a closed tart, looked hopeful. I rushed straight to the kitchen and made it, without its top and with a few adjustments. Good though it was, it wasn't right. The candied peel made it too like a mince tart, and where was the gooey, honeyed texture? The next day I tried again. I've no idea if this version is the real McCoy, but it looks like it, it was delicious in its own right, and everyone who ate it for Sunday lunch said they'd definitely eat it again.

Canadian Pie

Serves 6

Shortcrust Pastry (see page 158), baked blind in a 22 cm/9 inch round tin with a removable base
4 heaped tbsp golden syrup
1½ tbsp clear honey
25 g/1 oz butter
1 egg, beaten
2–3 tbsp double cream
150 g/5 oz currants
25 g/1 oz ground almonds
¼–½ tsp mixed spice
¼ tsp grated nutmeg
grated rind of 1 lemon
3 tsp lemon juice

Preheat the oven to 190°C/375°F/Gas Mark 5. Heat the golden syrup, honey and butter in a saucepan until liquid. Remove from the heat and stir in the beaten egg and the cream. Mix together all the other filling ingredients in a bowl, pour in the golden syrup mixture and stir well. Pour into the pastry case and cook in the oven for about 25 minutes, until nicely puffed up and browned. Serve with cream.

Shortcrust Pastry

MAKES ENOUGH TO LINE A 22 CM/9 INCH ROUND TART TIN

175 g/6 oz plain white or wholemeal flour
pinch of salt
85 g/3 oz butter, chilled

Sift the flour and salt into a bowl and grate in the butter, straight from the fridge. Using your fingertips, rub in the butter with the minimum of handling. Add just enough ice-cold water to bind the mixture together. Wrap in greaseproof paper and chill in the fridge for at least 20 minutes.

Roll out and line the tart tin, then chill in the fridge for another 20–30 minutes before baking in a preheated oven.

To bake blind, cut a circle of greaseproof paper to fit inside the pastry case, and fill it with baking beans (dried beans reserved for this purpose) to prevent the pastry from rising in the heat of the oven. Bake for about 10–15 minutes, then remove the paper and beans and bake for a further 5–10 minutes, depending on the recipe.

To make a larger amount of pastry, increase the flour and butter proportionately. So, for example, for 325 g/12 oz flour you will need 175 g/6 oz butter.

Sweet Pastry

MAKES ENOUGH TO LINE A 20 CM/8 INCH ROUND TART TIN

225 g/8 oz plain white flour
175 g/6 oz butter, softened
65 g/2½ oz caster sugar
2 egg yolks

I like to make this by simply placing all the ingredients in the food processor and pulsing for as short a time as possible, just until the mixture begins to come together in large crumbs. Wrap in greaseproof paper and chill in the fridge for at least 30 minutes.

If you do not have a food processor sift the flour on to a work surface and make a well in the centre. Put the butter, sugar and egg yolks in the well and then, using your fingertips, work them together until evenly mixed. Working quickly and lightly, incorporate the flour to form an even dough. Wrap and chill for at least 30 minutes.

Roll out and line the tart tin, then chill in the fridge for another 20–30 minutes before baking in a preheated oven.

It is New Year 1997 in the west of Ireland. The ground is iron hard, the stream behind the house half flowing, half iced over. The water pipes are frozen across the land, and have been for a week. We collect water by wheelbarrow with a bin and a bucket twice daily, baths and washing machine already a fading memory. My brother Daniel and his new wife Rebecca have just left with our friend Tor Belfrage. After a riotous New Year's Eve, the following evening found the four of us hysterical with laughter as we slid up the icy hill to the stream to replenish the commodity we are used to taking for granted – particularly in the west of Ireland which is wet in all seasons. Gloved, booted, hatted, we feel like frontierspeople from a bygone age, in a landscape whose beauty is preserved, like the bog, largely unchanged since my childhood holidays here.

Our family remain, John and I and our three children, Miranda, Harry and Charissa before the long journey back to England next week.

My thanks to them for testing and testing again the recipes that made this book and for their constant greed, criticism and approval.

My thanks also to the following, who are listed according to the rules of all plays, in the order in which they appeared. Firstly Georgina Capel, my agent, who ignored my cries of 'I can't write it', and sold it anyway. She is never one to miss the tiniest seed of an idea, even if it hasn't had time to germinate, so credit to her in no small measure. Next to Anthony Cheetham to whom George took the idea and with whom I discussed the original outline in the most creative and unprescriptive way. As a result, the original concept turned very quickly into something more ambitious, the accompanying pictures went from black and white to colour, and the book began to find a life of its own immediately. On meeting Michael Dover to discuss the concept I was steered briskly, but not forcefully, to Michael's preferred choice of photographer. All I can say is that Michael's advice and attention to detail have been invaluable and perfectly judged, and never righter than with his insistence on Simon Wheeler, the photographer. I will always see Simon as someone for whom the light is not quite right, the day never long enough, the mirage of perfection always hovering a breath away. The joy, though, of working with a perfectionist. The results I think are in themselves evidence of his talent and his ability to capture the mood, look, place, energy of all and every situation I put him in and many more besides. We pretty quickly shared the same vision of how text and pictures should marry, and I think the union was harmoniously accomplished!

Thanks also to the home economist Joy Davies for translating my recipes with such skill and perfection into pictures. Nigel Soper as graphic designer enhanced and artfully and enthusiastically translated our idea of the look, and has been a delight to work with. The layout of text and picture has been gone over with a fine toothcomb, and he has always found the best solution. Beth Vaughan has helped look after the emergent book over the last few months with patience, tolerance and good humour, and Maggie Ramsay has had the unenviable task of making sense of both text and recipes, and has worked extremely hard at interpreting the latter, and knocking them into their most assimilable form for the reader. Deborah Fox is, as always, first and last on all projects, her criticism, candour, calm and typing exemplary.

Recipe Index

Aillade 136
Aïoli 92
almonds: Peach and Almond Crumble Tart 74
anchovies: Anchovy and Caper Sauce 96
Anchovy Dressing 104
Red Onion Pissaladière 53
apples: Apple Sauce 123
Spiced Apple Pie 57
apricots: Hazelnut and Apricot Tart 113
artichokes: Beetroot, Broad Bean, Artichoke and Smoked Bacon Salad with an Anchovy Dressing 104
aubergines: Caponata 97
avocado: Cucumber and Avocado Sambal 67

bacon: Boiled Bacon with Cabbage 82
beans: Beetroot, Broad Bean, Artichoke and Smoked Bacon Salad with an Anchovy Dressing 104
Fasoulia 106
Flageolet Bean Casserole 38
Flageolet Beans 37
Green Beans in an Egg and Lemon Sauce 106
Béchamel Sauce 66, 153
Beef Braised with Guinness 12
beetroot: Baked Beetroot with Sour Cream 137
Beetroot, Broad Bean, Artichoke and Smoked Bacon Salad with an Anchovy Dressing 104
blackcurrants: Blackcurrant Leaf Sorbet 71
Blackcurrant Jelly 24
Brûléed Blackcurrant Tart 72
Raw Blackcurrant Fool 70
Raw Blackcurrant Ice Cream 70
Raw Blackcurrant Mousse 70
Brandy Butter 122
Bread Sauce 119
Brussels sprouts, Gratin of 137
Butterscotch Tart 17

cabbage: Boiled Bacon with Cabbage 82
Cabbage with Green Chillies and Turmeric 146
Colcannon 14
Dolmades Made with Cabbage Leaves 55
Canadian Pie 157
capers: Anchovy and Caper Sauce 96
Caper Sauce 36
Caponata 97
Carrots Vichy 89
Cauliflower with Roasted Cumin 145
Champ 40
cheese: Mozzarella-Stuffed Meatballs with Fresh Tomato Sauce 148
Watercress and Blue Cheese Salad with a Toasted Sesame Dressing 107
chestnuts: Chestnut Stuffing 117
Chocolate and Chestnut Terrine 131
chicken: Bourride of Chicken 91
Chicken in a Fruity Barbecue Sauce 48
Chicken in a Ginger and Yoghurt Paste 144
Chicken Smothered in Garlic 89
Poulet Vallée d'Auge 90
Chicken Liver Sauce, Pasta 154
chicory: Braised Endives 96
chocolate: Chocolate and Chestnut Terrine 131
Chocolate Sauce 129
Frozen Chocolate Parfait 129
Miranda's Chocolate Birthday Cake 134
Old-Fashioned Steamed Chocolate Pudding 130
Rich Chocolate Fondant 128
Wholewheat Chocolate Hazelnut Cake 132
Christmas Pudding 120
Colcannon 14
Courgettes, Sautéed 89
crab: Crab Soufflé with a Cucumber and Avocado Sambal 66
Crabcakes with Herb Mayonnaise 68
Souffléd Crab Tart 64
Cracked Wheat Salad 49
Cucumber and Avocado Sambal 67
Cumberland Sauce 109

Dal 146
Dolmades Made with Cabbage Leaves 55

eggs: Egg and Lemon Sauce 106
Herb Mayonnaise 68
Orange-Flower Sabayon 75
Tricolour Omelette 47
Endives, Braised 96

Fasoulia 106
fennel: Braised Fennel 64
Fennel Soufflé 67

goose: Roast Goose with Potato, Sage and Goose Liver Stuffing, and Apple Sauce 123

haddock: Mildly Curried Kedgeree 150
Smoked Haddock and Watercress Tart 151
ham: Salade Cauchoise 105
Hare: Civet of Hare with an Aillade 136
hazelnuts: Hazelnut and Apricot Tart 113
Wholewheat Chocolate Hazelnut Cake 132
herbs: Herb Mayonnaise 68
Herb Tart 152
Homity Pies 49
Honey and Lavender Ice Cream 74

Irish Stew 14
Italian Meat Loaf 46

Kedgeree, Mildly Curried 150

lamb: Braised Lamb Shanks with Champ 40
Dolmades Made with Cabbage Leaves 55
Irish Stew 14
Lamb Boulangère 38
Lamb's Liver, Roast 83
lavender: Honey and Lavender Ice Cream 74
leeks: Leek, Potato and Oatmeal Tart 87
Prawn and Leek Lasagne 153
lemons: Cumberland Sauce 109
Egg and Lemon Sauce 106
Lemon Tart 112-13
Tasmanian Lemon Pie 17
lentils: Dal 146
Lentil, Tomato and Pasta Soup 155
Loganberry Jam 24

mackerel: baked 32
Marinated Mackerel with Potato Salad 50
Madeira Cake 27
marmalade: Seville Orange and Marmalade Tart 124
Mayonnaise, Herb 68
Meat Loaf, Italian 46
Meatballs, Mozzarella-Stuffed, with Fresh Tomato Sauce 148
Mincemeat 121
Mushrooms, Baked Stuffed 107
mussels: Killary Bay Mussel Chowder 85
Mustard Sauce 138
mutton: Mutton Braised in Brandy and White Wine 37
Roast Mutton and Caper Sauce 36

oatmeal: Leek, Potato and Oatmeal Tart 87
Omelette, Tricolour 47
onions: Baked Onions 14
Red Onion Pissaladière 53
Orange-Flower Sabayon 75
oranges: Cumberland Sauce 109
Fresh Orange Jelly 122
Rhubarb, Orange and Honey Pie 57
Seville Orange and Marmalade Tart 124

pasta: Lentil, Tomato and Pasta Soup 155
Pasta in a Chicken Liver Sauce 154
Prawn and Leek Lasagne 153
peaches: Peach and Almond Crumble Tart 74
Poached Peaches in an Orange-Flower Sabayon 75
Peas, Stewed 77
Pistou 156
pollack: Mildly Curried Kedgeree 150
Scallop, Pollack and Squid Pie 30
pork: Rillettes de Tours 105
potatoes: Champ 40
Colcannon 14
Crisp Roast Potatoes 119
Garlic Mashed Potatoes 32
Leek, Potato and Oatmeal Tart 87
Potato Mayonnaise 109
Potato Salad 50
Roasted Rosemary Potatoes 68
Saffron Potatoes 64
Poulet Vallée d'Auge 90
Prawn and Leek Lasagne 153

Rabbit Stewed with Thyme in a Mustard Sauce 138
Rhubarb, Orange and Honey Pie 57
rice: Mildly Curried Kedgeree 150
Seafood Risotto 86
Spiced Rice Salad 108
Rillettes de Tours 105
Rouille 92

Saffron Potatoes 64
Salade Cauchoise 105
salmon: Ceviche of Salmon 108
Salmon Baked in Pastry with Currants and Ginger 76, 77
Scallop, Pollack and Squid Pie 30
Seafood Risotto 86
Shortcrust Pastry 158
Skate with an Anchovy and Caper Sauce 96
soda breads 26-7
Soupe au Pistou 156
squid: Scallop, Pollack and Squid Pie 30
Sweet Pastry 158

Tasmanian Lemon Pie 17
tomatoes: Fresh Tomato Sauce 149
Lentil, Tomato and Pasta Soup 155
Provençale Tomato Salad 87
Raw Tomato Sauce 148
Tricolour Omelette 47
Turkey, Roast, with Chestnut Stuffing 118

Vanilla Ice Cream 69

Walnut Biscuits 71
watercress: Smoked Haddock and Watercress Tart 151
Watercress and Blue Cheese Salad with a Toasted Sesame Dressing 107
Whitecurrant Jelly 24